Praise for
101 Ways to Help Your Daughter
Love Her Body

"This book is an extraordinarily useful guide to helping girls overcome body angst. It's also an illuminating cultural commentary on the social pressures that make growing up in a female body so difficult and complex in the twenty-first century."
  —Joan Jacobs Brumberg, author of *The Body Project: An Intimate History of American Girls* and *Fasting Girls: The History of Anorexia Nervosa*

"Every parent or educator who is serious about nurturing girls should read this book. It is so right-on about girls and how they see their bodies."
  —Maureen O'Toole, mother and silver-medal winner, water polo, 2000 Olympics

"A must-read for parents of girls—from toddlers to teens. This groundbreaking guide offers wise and practical strategies for helping girls wade through the perilous waters of childhood and adolescence. From Barbie to boyfriends, from mirrors to magazines, from sports to self-esteem, this book is full of relatable anecdotes and real-world solutions for raising healthy daughters in today's culture."
  —Lori Gottlieb, author of *Stick Figure: A Diary of My Former Self*

"This compassionate and intelligent guide is for any adult who wants to teach a girl to treat her body lovingly. I highly recommend it."
  —Genevieve Ferrier, M.D., pediatrician

"There are things we can do to affect our daughters' sense of self. Here is a much needed and excellently organized guide for parents of teenage girls."
  —Kenny and Julia Loggins

101
Ways to Help
Your Daughter
Love Her Body

101
Ways to Help
Your Daughter
Love Her Body

Brenda Lane Richardson and Elane Rehr

Quill

An Imprint of HarperCollins*Publishers*

HarperCollins books may be purchased for educational, business, or sales promotional use. For information please write: Special Markets Department, HarperCollins Publishers Inc., 10 East 53rd Street, New York, NY 10022.

FIRST EDITION

Designed by Joseph Rutt

Library of Congress Cataloging-in-Publication Data is available.

ISBN 0-06-095667-4

01 02 03 04 05 WB/RRD 10 9 8 7 6 5 4 3 2 1

With love from Mom to Carolyn, who plans to become the first fiction-writing, sketching, surfing, snowboarding, skateboarding, guitar-, soccer-, and volleyball-playing president of the United States.

And with love from Mom to Danielle, whose courage and iron will have allowed her to overcome life's greatest tests, and who will continue to overcome life's hurdles and inspire others. You love life, and it shows!

ACKNOWLEDGMENTS

Brenda Lane Richardson

This book could not have been written without the vision and hard work of Gail Winston, senior editor for HarperCollins. I am also enormously grateful for the assistance of my husband, the Reverend Doctor W. Mark Richardson, for my sons, H.P. and Mark Jr., and my daughter, Carolyn, and for the wisdom and courage of Elane Rehr. I am also grateful for the intelligence, good humor, and diligence of editorial assistant Christine Walsh.

Elane Rehr

I would like to acknowledge the tremendous endurance of Brenda Lane Richardson, who persevered through every rewrite and bump in the road, and of Gail Winston, our editor, who gave us crucial feedback and motivation. I would also like to thank my husband, Howard Davis, and my son, Deren, for all their love and support.

CONTENTS

Complete as the perfect wings of the jay above your head or the pale stars that mark your birth with nothing but pure light. Daughter, I cannot give you anything so complete or perfect or pure. But I can give you something better. Your body . . . And the fierce love of it that no one can take away. And these words will remind you of that love.

From "History of the Body,"
by Linda Nemec Foster,
anthologized in
I Am Becoming the Woman I've Wanted

INTRODUCTION

Why Our Daughters
Need Our Help

As the mothers of adolescent daughters, we started this book long before we ever put words on a page. We met in 1994, when our daughters were in the same third-grade class in Piedmont, California, and quickly discovered that our interests dovetailed. For more than thirty years, Elane has taught women's psychology and adolescent psychology at Diablo Valley College, while Brenda, a journalist since 1970, has written five self-help psychology books.

Like so many parents, we were concerned over reports of plunging self-esteem among adolescent girls—in large part as a result of the societal pressures on the female body—and we worried about how our daughters would be affected by this phenomenon. We know the problem isn't limited to girls and that in Western society in general, there is too much emphasis on looks. But body-image issues are more widespread among girls—and the problem only seems to be growing. At a time when their opportunities seem unlimited, girls can easily be constrained by a constant focus on the exterior.

We knew that despite our best efforts to convince our daughters that they could achieve anything, the societal chipping away at their body image could take a toll on their self-esteem. For that reason, we became invested in the pertinent literature and attended book readings, workshops, and parent discussion groups. But we were disappointed to discover that in most conversations about girls' self-esteem, other than a few timeworn ideas, the recommendations generally stopped short of the body. We interpreted this dearth of practical suggestions as a grudging acceptance by professionals that when it comes to girls, issues concerning the body are practically inevitable.

We couldn't accept this sorry state of affairs, especially in the face of all that works against girls loving their bodies. Consider the daily onslaught of more than a thousand visual and auditory commercial messages a day. A girl walks into a store and sees a magazine rack filled with publications displaying scantily-clad, computer manipulated images of half-starved female bodies with long, shapely legs. A bus drives by with a movie placard of a gray-haired actor in a suit, his twenty-something "leading lady" crouched at his feet; high above is a three-story billboard for Banana Republic. And home is not necessarily a refuge, but an extension of this commercial bombardment. One television advertisement may pitch a high-fat fast food, while the next pushes a weight-loss product. In a prime-time teenage drama, a fat girl is targeted for the punch line, while a slender actress portrays a seductress. The Internet and the radio only add to the confusion, with songs such as Matchbox 20's "Push," about a girl who has been pushed around.

We were determined to find a way to guide our daughters—who are so filled with enthusiasm and spirit—through the societal maze. And we knew that the notion of self-esteem is only an empty term if it doesn't include maintaining a love of the body. When we refer to body love or body esteem, we aren't talking about narcissism. Learning to love one's body means treating it respectfully, making peace with one's unique physique, and, yes, reveling in a sense of physical competence. Body esteem allows girls to act with self-direction and create lives that have meaning. It isn't about continuous good feeling or unwavering self-satisfaction, but it does allow a girl to view her internal strengths, rather than her appearance, as a projection of her worth. It allows her to retain an internalized image of her body as whole and wholesome, rather than as a package of distorted parts that must be dressed up and displayed to their best advantage.

Year after year, as we continued devising practical solutions for our girls, we knew we were on the right track, for they remained confident, passionate, and filled with joy. Then life sent us the biggest challenge of all. In 1999, Elane's daughter, Danielle, was diagnosed with a highly aggressive form of leukemia. At one point, her outcome looked so grim that

Danielle was sent home from the hospital to spend two weeks surrounded by people she loved, in the event that she died during her transplant. Brenda phoned Elane to suggest that they postpone what, by now, had become their manuscript. After all, Brenda reasoned, why worry about a book at a time such as this?

But Elane insisted on continuing their work. She said, "This book is more than just an interesting thesis. It's about how we strengthened our girls so that nothing—not society or other people or even we—could wear them down with ideas about what they're *supposed* to look like and be like. We wanted to protect them from obvious threats, like drugs, alcohol, sex, and the craziness about weight. But now that Danielle's caught up in this fight, I realize that in helping them love their bodies, we also helped them maintain their spirits. That's why Danielle is going to beat this disease."

We're happy to say that Elane was right. Danielle's cancer is in remission. She has returned to school and to her soccer team, and has added competitive swimming, as well as a more rigorous academic and social schedule, to her calendar. But she has done more than recover. Danielle's courage and vivaciousness was the impetus for a local volunteer effort that helps other adolescents with life-threatening illnesses.

Brenda's daughter, Carolyn, who is also fifteen, has faced struggles of a different sort, including her family's 1999 cross-country move from their safe and pristine northern California town to a new home in the middle of New York City. Feeling out of control and grieving over the loss of her long-term friendships, Carolyn soothed herself by overeating, and began to struggle with her weight. Fortunately, Carolyn has benefited from many of the techniques included in this work, and has identified and worked through the issues that fueled her emotional overeating. She is once again fit, active, and filled with a zest for life.

No matter what challenges your daughter may ultimately face, we believe she needs your help. Our girls are simply not equipped to handle the pressure of growing up in a society in which the female body is treated like an object. Jean Kilbourne, who researches the media's effect on self-image, believes that we inevitably value human beings less if we're surrounded by objectified representations of them. Kilbourne explains that "the first step towards justifying violence against a human being is to think of that person as less than human, to think of that person as an object."[1]

Objectification may be one explanation for why girls and women are frequently targeted for sexual violence. Two striking examples of violence against women captured national headlines: In June 2000, on a Sunday afternoon in New York's Central Park, more than fifty women, including at least two teenage girls, ages fourteen and sixteen, were heckled, chased, and in some cases groped, stripped, and sodomized by groups of frenzied young men.[2] The victims were targeted because of their gender. Some young men from the crowd acted as self-designated "scouts," alerting the larger group to women they deemed sexually appealing.[3]

Seven months later, in a spate of alleged incidents outside of New York City, police officers—in Nassau and Suffolk Counties, and in the town of Wallkill—were accused of stopping women drivers they deemed attractive and forcing them to disrobe or engage in oral sex; other women said they were sodomized or raped. A criminal justice professor described the alleged incidents as cases of DWF, driving while female.[4]

Across the country, countless more Americans participate in private, consensual versions of dramas in which the message is much the same: Women are sexual objects for the enjoyment and pleasure of men. In one affluent northern California city, despite pressure from disapproving parents and education officials, an unsavory tradition continues, the so-called Pimp and Ho Party. High school girls dress to look like prostitutes, and the boys, swaggering and full of macho energy, pretend they are their pimps. Although many of these girls hail from some of the "best" families, it should not be surprising that they submit to such mistreatment. Psychologists have long known about a phenomenon called "identification with the enemy," in which those who are mistreated begin to adopt the views and attitudes of those who mistreat them. For this reason alone, self-abnegation runs rampant among our daughters.

In Raleigh, North Carolina, thirteen-year-old Samantha*— pencil slim, with a face full of freckles—claims she has tried dozens of diets because "I hate it when my butt starts looking like a hog's. At the end of the winter, I usually have to start wearing my fat shorts, which are size four." To get back into "model shape," Samantha jogs with her mom at dawn seven days a week and keeps herself motivated with pictures of pop princess Britney Spears, taped to her mirror. Samantha added, "When I get bigger than Britney, I know my body is looking gross."

She certainly isn't alone when it comes to feeling the need to measure herself against images presented in the media. A few years ago, Sara Shandler, then sixteen, grew concerned about how commercial images were negatively affecting her and her peers. Her sensibilities had been heightened by Mary Pipher's best-seller, *Reviving Ophelia*, which sounded the alarm on the "poisoning" effects of the media, materialism, and the insecurities of adolescent girls. Shandler contacted other teenagers around the country and asked them to write about their struggles for a book she hoped to compile. When letters began to pour in, for what eventually became the best-selling *Ophelia Speaks*, Shandler found that without any prompting, twenty young women sent essays that addressed the pathological environment created by the bombardment of visual images of "perfect" bodies.[5]

Their concerns are validated by several studies in the field of body-image research that have linked growing dissatisfaction

---

*For the sake of privacy, when necessary, we have changed the names and biographical details of individuals whose stories are shared in this book.

with appearance to the ultra-thin bodies reflected in the media. In fact, it seems that wherever Western magazines, billboards, movies, and television are found, so, too, is the drive to be reed thin.[6] One study found no instances of eating disorders among Egyptian women studying in Cairo universities, but when researchers looked at Egyptian women studying in England—where there is also a visual bombardment of commercial images—they found that 12 percent met the criteria for disordered eating.[7] And when television shows that had been produced in the West were introduced in the Fiji Islands, there was an increase in eating disorders.[8] In the United States, an estimated one in six teenage girls has symptoms of eating disorders such as bulimia or anorexia.[9] Though these girls are labeled "sick" for seeing themselves as "fat," they are actually responding to society's distorted perception of what girls and women are *supposed* to look like.

The media is not entirely to blame. The thin norm is so ubiquitous that it seems that even the most casual acquaintances feel free to pressure girls about their bodies. We heard a story in St. Louis about seventeen-year-old Sissy, whose friends stood in awe at the junior prom as Javier, the hottest boy in town, asked her to dance. Sissy thought she was dreaming as Javier pulled her in closer for their cheek-to-cheek. But romance wasn't in the picture. Javier whispered to Sissy, "I asked you to dance so I could tell you to suck in your stomach. It's sticking out."

The attack against the female body is so pervasive in Western culture that it has already affected the relationship of newly arrived Russian immigrants Sasha, age thirty-two, and her fourteen-year-old sister. Sasha, who shed twenty pounds within six months of her arrival in the United States, says, "My little sis has fleshy arms and thighs ribboned with cellulite." When she watched her baby sister dress for a date, Sasha was shocked that their mother encouraged the girl to wear a short-sleeved minidress. Sasha intervened, telling her sister to "cover up her fat." Her sister cried and pushed Sasha out of the room. "She acted like I was the one who was crazy," said Sasha.

We found, not surprisingly, that most conversations concerning a girl's body occur between mother and daughter. In Michigan, Doris, a salesclerk, is delighted that her twelve-year-old-daughter, Kim, who "tends naturally to be on the chunky side," is concerned about how to keep thin. Kim drinks a can of Slimfast at lunchtime and then rushes to the community pool to work off the calories. Doris says, "I've taught her to be careful about her weight. This can be a tough world when you're fat."

Conversations such as these affect even young girls. In one study, Joan Chrisler, a psychology professor at Connecticut College, found that 68 percent of fifth graders said they were scared of being fat.[10] The problem is that although we love our girls and have their best interests at heart, so many of us think of our own bodies as flawed that today's men and women may be ill equipped to help their girls love their bodies. How can we teach girls to love their bodies when we haven't learned to love our own?

This is a relatively new social phenomenon. When our grandmothers were young, their ideas about what they should look like tended to be more clearly tied to reality. There was certainly an interest in dieting at the start of the twentieth century, but character and a young woman's inner beauty were still stressed more than outer appearance. It was a different world from the one we live in today.

Our grandmothers had close extended families and stable communities filled with women of numerous body types. Of course, they also dreamed of romance and excitement, but those dreams were encouraged via literature and the radio. These images were more a product of the individual's imagination. As listeners and readers pictured a heroine, they adapted that image to a wide range of body types based on the women in their lives—tall, buxom, self-assured aunts; portly sisters with a bloom in their cheeks; a favorite teacher who was feather light.

Those images narrowed as Hollywood sought out a body type that would look good on the silver screen and eventually on television, media that make actors appear about fifteen pounds heavier than they actually are. Some of us came of age when there was pressure to be full bodied, like Marilyn Monroe (who, although curvaceous, was actually much smaller in person than most fans realized. In the 1990s, when some of Monroe's vintage items were auctioned, they were too small for some size-eight women). By the time today's mothers of teenagers reached adolescence, dictates had changed. The popularity of fashion models was growing, and Twiggy had become a role model, as well as a legion of boyish-framed starlets.

The media now promotes a look that can catch the eye to sell a product. With heights of five feet seven inches or taller and weights between 100 and 110 pounds, fashion models are about 23 percent thinner than 75 percent of American women, who weigh, on the average, about 143 pounds and are five feet four inches or shorter.

Although many of us are aware of these realities, we have remained locked in battle with our bodies. And since the ideal body has continued to get slimmer, it's a battle that's hard to win. Consider the thinning down of Miss America. Since 1921, the average Miss America's weight has decreased 12 percent. And sometime in the mid-1970s, the average winner's body mass index (BMI) fell below 18.5, a level considered unhealthy by the World Health Organization. (The BMI score reflects a person's weight divided by height to arrive at a number indicative of weight-related health.[11])

It may be that only a few of these contestants come by their slender bodies naturally. In 1979, the average Miss America contestant exercised fourteen hours per week, and some as much as thirty-five hours a week.[12] These women certainly can't be blamed for being preoccupied with thinness. Even though medical research suggests that it's more risky to be 15 percent underweight than 15 percent overweight, according to Western dictates underweight is equated with good health.

This is not simply a woman's issue. An increasing number of men also work hard at remaining trim and buff. But the obsession to meet strident standards is largely a woman's struggle. In a 1985–86 study of 260 students at UCLA, 27.3 percent of the women, but only 5.8 percent of the men, said they were "terrified" of becoming fat. Thirty-five percent of the women versus 12.5 percent of the men said they felt fat even though other people told them they were thin. The women also wanted to weigh ten pounds under their average weight, while the men said they were within a pound of the weight they hoped for.[13]

Unfortunately, body obsessiveness is passed from mother to daughter. Fathers also play an important role in their daughters' relationships with food and their bodies. Researchers have linked severe weight problems in young children with parents who dieted constantly and binged.[14] But because mothers and daughters share the same body parts, it is mothers who have the most profound psychological influence on the way girls view their bodies. It stands to reason that they also have the potential to affect positively their daughters' body image, but it doesn't always happen that way.

Roxanne, age thirty-six, a plump media executive, has an eleven-year-old daughter who is thirty pounds overweight. "I'm in such a panic about her that I'm thinking of staying home to control what she's eating. When I try to talk to her about how big she's gotten, she snaps at me," Roxanne confided.

Food conflicts were the last thing Roxanne wanted. As a child, Roxanne argued with her own mother over food and when she closes her eyes, she can still hear her mom saying, "No more. You've had enough!" She eventually grew into an overweight child. All these years later, here was her daughter, weighing more perhaps than Roxanne did at the same age. Roxanne sighed. "I don't get it. She has grown up seeing me struggle to lose weight. Why would she do this to herself, and why won't she accept my help now before it's too late?" Like Roxanne, many women feel dissatisfied with their daughters' bodies and are frustrated that they are unable to make life easier for them. Though they may try to see their daughters as separate individuals, many project themselves onto their daughters' experiences.

Fathers, too, get involved in family body wars, sometimes cruelly teasing their daughters or initiating confrontations, as well as employing more covert approaches. Several women told us of arguments they have had with husbands who are angry that their daughters are not thin enough. Kenneth, age forty-three, admits that when his son was overweight, he reassured him that if he continued participating in sports and eating properly, his body would turn out "just perfect." By age twelve, the boy was indeed tall and slender—as befitted his body type. But when his daughter grew husky, Kenneth came undone. "Her extra weight reminded me of being a kid with a fat mother. It was so embarrassing. One kid used to hold his nose when she went by. I have never dated a fat woman, and to be honest, watching my daughter eat can make me ill. I threw out every cookie, potato chip, and soft drink. Next, I'm getting rid of the television. I'm sick of the inactivity. My wife says I'm crazy. I admit it. I'm not rational about our daughter's size."

In generations past, families battled over a daughter's virginity. Today's skirmishes may center on a girl's size. In either case, the daughters are the ones who are being hurt by their parents' tendency to view them as reflections of their social status or to judge them by their clothing size. Parental pressures to slim down may involve a mother or father criticizing their own bodies or those of others, in the secret hope that their daughters will get the message and remain slim.

Ironically, the more a child feels pressured to slim down, the more she may overeat to stave off the sense of being unloved and unaccepted. We aren't suggesting that the solution is to let children eat without reservation. We believe young people should be encouraged to be healthy and fit. But one need only look at statistics to see that the pressure to remain "model thin" isn't paying off. Although a lot of the focus in the body image field is justifiably paid to girls who risk their lives under-eating, an even greater number of girls are affected by overeating. An estimated 6 million children are heavy enough for their health to be endangered, and about five million more are on the threshold of obesity.[15] We are not talking about youngsters being just "a little heavier" than their counterparts from the past. In the United States, the prevalence of childhood obesity increased by 100 percent from 1980 to 1994.[16] This book is not a diet guide, but it would have been impossible to approach the subject of body esteem without stressing the need for a healthy lifestyle, and that includes teaching girls to enjoy eating in a manner that reflects self-love. Being at peace with one's body leaves little room for self-punishment, whether through under- or overeating, the use of harmful substances, or engaging in risky behaviors.

It seems that parents are always asking for advice on what they can say to their daughters about being overweight. Many of these parents have been in terrible pain, but "have never said a word" to their girls because they don't want to hurt them. However, when a situation is fraught with conflict, silence is never an appropriate response. In this weight-conscious society, children know when they are considered overweight, and they certainly know when their parents see them that way. Since every family has a unique situation, we can't give you the "right" words, but we have designed suggestions that pave the way to the most intimate body conversations. By engaging in this work, you will be creating a changed emotional environment in your home that will enable your daughter freely to initiate conversations about her body. And you will feel confident that you have the right answers.

We have addressed this book of suggestions and activities to mothers, but we urge you not to use it as one more reason to live your life in overdrive. We have also included specific suggestions for fathers and hope they will read the work in its entirety. Fathers are not only important in children's care and upbringing, but, like mothers, they have exclusive contributions to make with regard to the way their daughters view themselves. Other suggestions are designed to help your daughter create a lifestyle that is conducive to maintaining a healthy body—in other words, to help her treat her body lovingly. Many suggestions don't require doing anything so much as they require a change in attitude. But there are also several activities your daughter can enjoy on her own or with other adults in her life, including older sisters, grandparents, godparents, relatives, friends, child care providers, teachers, and youth workers. You may want to pencil the names of significant others alongside some suggestions to remind you of who may be the most help in a particular area. You will find that most people will get quite energized around the ideas presented in this work.

Why wouldn't they? For they, too, will be able to imagine the possibilities of sending young women into the world who feel just as confident about their bodies as they do about their professional skills. Imagine the power of young women moving through the world with self-possession. This is what the feminist movement has directed us toward. It is the transformation that *Reviving Ophelia* called for. Side by side with our own daughters, we urge you to join us in taking the next step.

101
Ways to Help
Your Daughter
Love Her Body

I

Beyond Lullabies
Teaching Body Comfort to Little Ones

It's true that the youngest children don't necessarily understand our words, but we know that they can read our body language and tone of voice and can even pick up on our reaction to them from the way we hold and touch them and the tone of our voices. The messages that they intercept during the first seven years of their lives are not forgotten; rather, they become part of an enduring pattern on their central nervous systems. That means we can give our little ones indelible memories of body comfort and tranquillity.

(1) Learn Baby Massage

As a mom, you already know there is nothing more comforting you can give your infant than your reassuring touch. It is by far your most intimate and powerful way of communicating love and reassurance. So why not improve upon something that you already know works?

Massage, which relieves tension, promotes blood flow, and calms the nervous system, will help your baby love being in her body right from the start. Thousands of parents have already learned baby massage, and you can too—applying loving touch to your daughter's skin, muscles, tendons, and ligaments.

"Sometimes when our little ones are crying, we try everything—changing the diaper, feeding, burping, rocking—but nothing seems to work," explained Christine Sutherland, a veteran massage practitioner in Nelson, British Columbia. She has taught scores of parents how to give their babies the deep-down comfort of trained touch. But Sutherland doesn't just teach baby massage, she practiced it on her daughter, Crystal. "I remember working on her little arms and legs, her back and feet, watching her relax, the tension flowing out of her. I knew she could feel my approval of her body on a level that didn't require intellectual skills."

There's research to indicate that Sutherland's motherly instincts are right on target. According to some studies, massage can lower levels of the stress hormone cortisol—which can help boost a baby's immune system. Massaged preemies have also been found to gain weight faster than nonmassaged ones.[1]

Parents of fretful babies may also opt for massage as a way of weaning infants six months and older from pacifiers. Studies have found an association between the continuous use of pacifiers and ear infections in children older than six months (although they are encouraged for helping younger babies fall asleep and for decreasing the risk of sudden infant death syndrome).[2]

Should you decide to learn baby massage, encourage your husband to join you. Some fathers have found that learning baby massage helped them feel more comfortable about holding their little ones. Your baby will feel more relaxed if her daddy is, too.

Sutherland's daughter is now a freshman in college, but she still looks forward to her mom's weekly massages. Sutherland said that during the teenage years, when Crystal's friends went through a period of obsessing over their physical features, "she was at peace about her body. She has no sense of being anything but beautiful." Sutherland credits her daughter's body acceptance to her early exposure to massage. "When a child experiences safe touch from someone she loves, it's a validation of her body." For much the same reason, massage has been found to be helpful in treating anorexia.

How can you learn baby massage? Ask your physician or a friend for recommendations for a massage therapist. Also, check with your health insurance carrier—some now cover massage treatments. Finally, check the Internet under "Baby Massage."

(2) Explore Fears of Baby Fat

Kara Lea, a mother in Louisville, Kentucky, winced when she recalled her husband's response to their daughter, who at the time was thirteen months old and chubby. "Steve bought her a toddler tricycle. He felt she needed to exercise. Now, this was a child who had been chubby since she was six months old and only surviving on breast milk. Her baby fat had nothing to do with overeating. But Steve kept joking that Rachel had thunder thighs and that she needed to work off the fat. He said that maybe there was a Richard Simmons tape for infants. I couldn't stop him with his damn fat jokes."

We can certainly understand Kara Lea's irritation, and we

can also understand her husband's fear, the emotion that drove him to make such insensitive jokes. In a society in which fat is an anathema, the most well-meaning parents tend to panic even over baby fat. That panic can become part of the emotional atmosphere in a home, affecting all occupants. Since even the youngest children can sense parental conflict, little Rachel may well have picked up on the fact that she caused tension between her parents. There is the additional problem of any feelings of rejection her father's responses may have engendered. Steve may have communicated his disapproval by holding her rigidly or occasionally frowning when he looked at her. No one would choose to convey such damaging messages to a child, but a great deal of one's behavior is determined by unconscious thoughts.

If you're concerned about your baby being fat, it may help you to know that researchers who examined the heights and weights of 854 people found that fat infants (those under age three) were no more likely to be fat adults than were babies of normal weights.[3] Simply put, fat babies don't necessarily become fat adults.

If baby fat is seen as a problem in your home, you should also know that a child who senses a parent's disapproval will feel emotionally abandoned. And children who are struggling with issues of abandonment often soothe themselves with food. This means that a parent's overreaction to an infant's body can contribute to future eating problems. You may also want to discuss the matter with your daughter's pediatrician. Rachel's physician assuaged some of Steve's fears by telling him about a study which found that infants who have been breast fed for a year or more, as Rachel was, are far less likely than formula fed babies to be obese by the time they begin grade school. (If you did not breast feed your baby, keep in mind that there are also millions of slender adults who were fed formula in infancy.)

What will surely not allay your fears about baby fat is to tell yourself not to think about it anymore. You may need emotional closure on the subject. Any overreaction to your daughter's body is a sign that she's putting you in touch with hurtful childhood experiences. For this reason you may want to explore your early memories, which may include a parent's rejection, a family drama that may have centered on you, or a parent or sibling's weight. One of the most effective methods for tapping into your unconscious is to write a letter that you will not send, addressing it first to one parent and then to the other. Your letter can begin "Dear Mom [or Dad], I am feeling critical of [your daughter's name]'s body, and this may be connected to my childhood experiences." Don't think about what you want to write, just let it rip. Your unconscious mind will drive you to keep writing and fill in some missing blanks. If none of your memories or emotions surface the first time, keep trying. Once you do identify hurtful events, images, or feelings, spend some time writing about them, and you should feel a sense of relief and, eventually, become more accepting of your baby's body.

Another approach to understanding any fears you may have about infant fat is to look over some of your early baby and family photos to jog your memory and, if possible, ask your parents to fill you in on significant details that you may have forgotten. Explain that you're not blaming them for your issues, but that you want to raise their granddaughter in the healthiest possible manner.

Finally, if it's a relative or friend who's suggesting that your baby is too chubby, tell this person that your child looks beautiful to you. If your daughter is lucky, you'll mean it.

(3) Dance with Her

When your girl is still an infant, hold her to you with one hand around her body, another supporting her head and neck, and gently sway to the music of your choice. Even the youngest of children will enjoy these musical playtimes. Regular patterned movement is naturally soothing to an infant. Don't forget that for months leading up to her birth she listened to the beat of your heart. And there are advantages to dancing with your baby girl. The body's sense of movement stems from the vestibular system—located inside the inner ears—and continues to mature between six and twelve months of age. The vestibular system needs to be stimulated. Dancing with your daughter can also enhance her motor development and help her learn faster. What's more, when your baby is tense and crying, your gentle rocking will help restore equilibrium to her nervous system so she can calm down and breathe better.[4]

When she becomes a toddler, after having taken some of her first uncertain steps away from you and then rushing back to the safety of your arms, she will love having you swoop her up and encircle her in your arms as you dance together. If your little girl is over age two and at a point in her life when she's feeling her separateness from you, she may not want you to hold her, but instead may prefer to have you bring out some toy instruments so the two of you can make your own music together. By this time in her life, she will be able to laugh along with her family. And she will certainly have much to laugh about. You are communicating to her that you take pleasure in your body, in all that it can do and express. As she matures and music becomes a dominant force in her life, sharing it with her in dance is one more way to retain an important connection. Years from now, when she dances with another partner, she will remember positively these early experiences and how the two of you celebrated your bodies.

(4) Get Her Out of the Stroller or Car Seat and Up on Her Own Two Feet

After our children have taken their first steps and the Kodak moment has passed, many of us—in our rush to get to the next pit stop—unwittingly teach our daughters that the best transportation is a stroller, car, or our arms. That's unfortunate, because walking, which could be called the original weight-bearing exercise, will not only enhance your daughter's motor and mental development but will also set the stage for an active, healthy lifestyle.[5] Besides, the human body is designed for self-propelled movement. Each time our feet hit the ground, we stimulate bone growth in our legs and hips.[6]

With these benefits in mind, the next time you're thinking about your trip to her preschool or when you have to run an errand, schedule in some extra minutes. Then, if safety permits, set her on her own two feet and let her rip. Chances are she'll not only want to walk, but run too. You'll know when you see her take off that even from this early age she is tuning in to her body's wisdom. Walking and running—there couldn't be more natural steps toward the health and self-care of her body.

(5) Encourage Dress-up and Playacting

Younger children love pretending that they are someone else and giving physical life to these fantasies. That's one reason (besides the candy) that so many children rank Halloween among their favorite occasions. Dressing up and playacting also appeal to young girls because of the glamour. And these activities can be enjoyed alone or with a group of other children. Although playacting is certainly not new, it is relevant in your effort to help your daughter love her body. You can use these times to make the point that what she puts on her body has little to do with who she is—that she is far more than what she wears.

Although there are mail-order companies that offer dress-up kits, with items that include feather boas, plastic pearl earrings, and vinyl high heels, you may want to ask your daughter's grandparents or godparents to put together a dress-up collection, adding stitches when necessary, to make adult clothing child sized. This is also something that the two of you may enjoy doing together. Pull out that old minidress and those hot pants or bell-bottoms you may have been holding on to, and add gloves, hats, shawls, and old pocketbooks. If she's still too small for your old clothes, shop for some that are closer to her size in used-clothing stores. Collect items that she can step into to act out several different personae.

For instance, one outfit alone may allow her to play a witch, Greek muse, cabaret dancer, angel, or any other character she decides to make up on the spot. Challenge her to come up with as many different personalities as possible while in the same outfit. Then point out how she has used her personality and talent to give her clothes life, and that it's not the other way around. Encourage her to name her favorite characters so you can refer to them later, as in "sounds like you're having a Miss Looney Tunes moment" or "I wonder how Princess Rogers would feel about that?" You will be reminding her that she is a complex and dynamic individual, someone who is far more than what can be seen on the outside. At some point she will want to pull you in on the act or perform for you. Dress-up is a wonderful way for both of you to have fun using your bodies— and minds.

(6) Reframe Barbie's Image

If your daughter asks for a Barbie doll, consider her request an opportunity to communicate the message that she has a body that's far superior to Barbie's. This can be a lot of fun if you remember not to preach, but to play. In reframing Barbie's image, it's important that you teach your daughter to be accepting of her, despite her disabilities. After all, Barbie has feet made only for high heels and hair so long that it often gets caught in fences and athletic nets.

Here's a possible play scenario: Barbie and a number of other more realistic dolls are setting up house. In addition to the plastic babe, you should let your daughter choose one with whom she strongly identifies. For the time being, we'll call her "Superdoll." She and Barbie and a few other friends are moving furniture into a dollhouse, carrying boxes (wooden blocks) and doll furniture. Oops! See Barbie trip. Those unrealistically high arches make it hard for her to walk back and forth, so Barbie has to sit and rest.

Superdoll and her friends are laughing and enjoying their physical selves. They relish one another's company and like to dance and sing along with their music. Later, Barbie—who has changed into a ball gown—is still sitting as Superdoll and her friends set up their computers. They are eager to hear from celebrities who are E-mailing them with invitations.

Marion Jones wants them to come out for a run; the entire U.S. Women's soccer team challenges them to a match, Venus and Serena Williams want to practice with them before the tennis quarterfinals. Everyone seems to be vying for Superdoll's time because the world appreciates girls who are filled with passion, who are in the middle of the action, and who enjoy their healthy, well-tuned bodies.

Meanwhile, here comes Barbie. She's on her way to a modeling audition, and she looks simply gorgeous. Superdoll and her friends give Barbie a great big cheer and lots of hugs. But Barbie soon returns crying. The photographer has turned her down. This year, he has told her, round hips are in, and hers tend to be less curvaceous. Superdoll and her friends try to comfort Barbie, but they can't stay up late. They need a good night's sleep for their exciting school day tomorrow.

As your daughter matures, explain through your "play" that Barbie has been designed so unrealistically, and so unlike a real woman—more like the computer-perfected images of models shown in magazines—that Barbie can't have as much fun and excitement in life as your daughter can.

(7) Encourage Her to Jump Rope

If ever there was a childhood activity that many of us recall with fondness, it is jumping rope. This activity evokes memories of times when junior schedules were not crammed with after-school activities, when long hours of homework were not required, and when children didn't spend most of their free time indoors before a television or computer screen.

You may not be able to duplicate these fun-filled afternoons for your daughter, but you can pass on the gift of jumping rope (even if you never tried it yourself). It's not only an affordable activity, but a healthy one. Jumping rope can build bone density and muscle power and provides a great aerobic workout.[7] Jumping rope is also an activity your daughter can engage in whether she's alone, with a sibling or pal, or a group of kids.

The best way to spark her interest in this activity is to jump rope with her or encourage her dad to do so (remind him that boxers often include jumping rope in their training). If you're lucky enough to have a basement or recreation room, not even inclement weather can interrupt your workouts. And if you are participating with your girl, you may want to know that if you can eventually work up to twenty-minute stretches, you're giving yourself an excellent cardiovascular workout. But don't think of it as work. Teach your daughter some of the ditties you may recall, like the ones about Miss Mary Mack, Cinderella dressed in yeller, or the lady with the alligator purse. If you've forgotten them, there are plenty of books available on the subject, including *Anna Banana: 101 Jump-Rope Rhymes*, by Joanna Cole.

(8) Turn Fairy-Tale Victims into Self-Rescuers

With descriptions that evoke the splendor of royal balls and sumptuous feasts and the excitement of seemingly impossible quests, fairy tales can transport reader and listener alike to magical times. In *The Uses of Enchantment*, child psychologist Bruno Bettelheim made the case that fairy tales can be powerful influences on children. In identifying with the story's victims, children realize that even people who are powerless (as children feel they are) can triumph over the most daunting circumstances. The big problem with traditional fairy tales, however, is that they tend to present heroines as helpless victims. That doesn't necessarily mean you should disavow fairy tales for your daughter. In fact, fairy tales can be tremendously helpful in boosting her sense of confidence in her body, if—while reading aloud—you make small plot changes that convey the message that girls are physically and emotionally empowered to save themselves.

There are no hard-and-fast rules in this approach. Simply put on your thinking cap when you see the main female character about to be portrayed as a victim. That's when you can substitute your own ideas for what's printed on the page.

Take the story of *Snow White*. You may change some details to endow the heroine with admirable traits. For instance, the stepmother may be jealous of Snow White because of her intelligence, not because she is beautiful. Snow White can convince the dwarfs to clean their home because of her excellent leadership skills. The prince finds Snow White in the woods because her fierce will to live shines like a beacon in the forest. In the story of *The Little Mermaid*, the main character could tell the witch that she would never give up her body to pursue the prince and goes along with that nonsense only because the witch casts a spell on her.

There are also a number of fairy-tale books available that celebrate the strengths of girls and women. Ask your librarian for references or shop on-line. One novel-length fairy tale with a strong female character is *Dealing with Dragons,* by Patricia C. Wrede, for ages nine through fourteen. There is also *Women Warriors: Myths and Legends of Heroic Women,* by Marianna Mayer, with beautiful illustrations by Julek Heller, for girls ages nine through fourteen. The twelve heroines highlighted in this culturally diverse book hail from countries that include Zimbabwe, India, and Japan.

Don't feel you have to abandon this approach when your daughter reaches adolescence. If you switch the focus to teen-oriented films, she will enjoy the sense of being in on the joke as she critiques some plots for you. You can only hope that she will see *Titanic,* for example, as a film about a girl who is bored stiff until she's rescued by an artist who shows her how to *really* live—which in this case, includes taking off her clothes so he can paint a picture of her in the nude.

II

Your Body, Your Self
Learning Self-Love So You Can Model It

As mothers, we've learned we're more likely to do for our children that which we've been unable to do for ourselves. That can be reassuring when we consider our own bodies. It's as if the universe is offering a fresh start—a new relationship with our bodies so we can begin a new conversation with our daughters.

(9) Give Her Permission to Love Her Body

Your first thought upon seeing a suggestion such as this may be, "Why would I want to tell her something that's so obvious?" This idea may begin to make sense only when you realize that giving your daughter permission to love her body can open the door to the kind of talk you wish you'd had with your mother. Think of it as an opportunity to engage in a truly intimate conversation with your daughter about early experiences that may have led you to mistrust, dislike, or become critical of your body. Point out to her how unrealistically slender images portrayed in the media often lead girls and women to feel shame about their own physiques. Depending on her age, your daughter may have many of her own thoughts to share with you. Continue by explaining that you hope her experiences can be more self-affirming than yours may have been, so she can truly treasure her body. Finally, urge her to object to any of your behaviors that may interfere with her loving her body.

Giving your daughter permission to love her body is similar to a mother who has been in a bad marriage telling her daughter that she hopes she will create a more loving relationship for herself. Sometimes children can feel so guilty about experiencing something better than their parents had that they unwittingly sabotage their own happiness, and, of course, you don't want that for your girl. When you give her permission to love her body, it's as if you're unlocking the doors to a castle and encouraging her to take possession.

(10) Model a Healthy Body Image

Many of our attitudes about our bodies were learned from our mothers. As we consider the legacy we want to pass on to our daughters, many of us are determined to change the way we respond to our own bodies. We know that if we are to help them feel peaceful about their bodies, we must model for them our own self-affirmation.

To get off to a good start, if you have engaged in any put-downs of your own body, decide right now to end this self-destructive behavior. You know what we mean. No more obsessively weighing yourself on the bathroom scale (weekly weighing is just fine, but be sure to do away with any groans or self-admonitions). Also put an end to complaints, such as, "I'm so flat chested" or "I hate my legs." When you catch yourself slipping, make a correction by saying something positive about the body part in question, such as, "I'm so grateful that my legs got me through that crowded store." It may sound false to you in the beginning, but after about thirty days (time for reprogramming your subconscious) you will discover that you are more likely to talk about yourself in a more affirming way. This also means that the next time someone gives you a compliment, rather than objecting—"No, I'm so fat"—you can take a deep breath and feel the kindness of the words all throughout your body.

This all becomes easier when you remind yourself that your body truly is a miracle. Consider the digestive system, which breaks down and distributes each morsel you eat more efficiently than a high-tech factory. And, of course, there is your heart, which continues to pump—even when you sleep—sending nutrients to every cell. Benefiting from these nutritional baths, your entire body, including your eyes and brain, work together, helping you to decipher the symbols on this page. Consider fostering an attitude of gratitude by taking a few moments each day to acknowledge various aspects of your body. One book that you may want to read is *Woman: An Intimate Geography,* by Natalie Angier. This beautifully written nonfiction work will make you proud of your female body.

You can reinforce this message for your daughter by taking

her along with you for annual visits to your gynecologist. When your girl is age thirteen to fifteen, she should begin visiting a gynecologist for annual checkups. Unfortunately, adolescent girls see doctors less than any other group of health care recipients.[1]

Don't be secretive about your intention to change your relationship with your body. Your daughter should be the first to know. She needs to hear you state what you've been doing wrong. Thinking out loud—or processing with your daughter—is a good idea. Here's an example of what you may say: "Honey, I just realized that I've been spending too much time putting my body down and not enough time congratulating it. Even though I weigh more than I wish I did, I eat healthy food and exercise regularly. I'm in good shape. What do you think?" She will probably have a lot to say on the matter.

(11) Don't Make Aging Sound Like a Curse

Another important aspect of modeling body affirmation is communicating to your daughter that your body is worthy and deserving of self-love and self-respect at any age. You may start with something as simple as calling your girl's attention to advertising campaigns that include vital older women, such as the series currently being run by the designer Eileen Fisher. This series of ads includes a gray-haired model devoid of heavy makeup, who truly could be the woman next door.

If you catch yourself engaging in any age-denigrating behaviors—such as griping about having one more birthday or refusing to tell people your age as if it were a shameful secret or moaning when you spot a gray hair or wrinkle—turn the statement around and say something positive. For example, perhaps you or your daughter have noticed that the veins in your hands are looking more prominent. You can remind her—and yourself—that those veins are just a few of your 62,000 miles of blood vessels, part of a circulatory system that delivers oxygen-rich blood throughout your body. No human-made transportation system even comes close to being this efficient. So while we aren't suggesting that you pretend to feel happy about aging, keep in mind that focusing on the miracle of your body can help you develop a new perspective.

This new perspective means disavowing the media message that when it comes to bodies, aesthetics are to be valued over function. Most of us wouldn't put up with that message if we were talking about our kitchens, so why in the world would we accept it for ourselves? When women are asked which older actresses have perfect bodies, they usually mention celebrities such as Goldie Hawn, Tina Turner, Cher, and Jane Fonda. What they and many of us fail to realize is that if we got our priorities in order—function *before* beauty—we would discover that *we* have perfect bodies. By this we mean bodies that have a good chance of remaining vital and healthy all the way through life.

George Ann Garms, of Berkeley, California, illustrates this point. If she stood beside Cher or Goldie Hawn, few people would label Garms, a slender wisp of a woman, a perfect ten. But at the age of seventy-six, with her erect posture and high-voltage stamina, this grandmother and widow could leave women half her age in the dust. In 1992, at a time when some of her contemporaries were discussing whether women should drive a car once they were widowed, Garms piloted her own plane to Siberia.

Garms believes that since so many women devote about twenty years of their lives to the care and nurturing of others, it isn't until after they're sixty that they can live their lives to their fullest. From this standpoint, it's just as important to have a body that feels youthful later in life as it is during your early years. Boy, does Garms put that theory to the test. During one recent vacation, this septuagenarian left behind her "gentleman-friend" and flew to Nevada, where she and a buddy rode horses into the mountains, then hiked and backpacked for five days. Garms, who is also a jewelry maker and graphic artist, credits her youthfulness to "good" eating and exercise.

So if you ever catch yourself moaning to your daughter about getting older, back off and tell her how lucky you both are to live at a time when so much is known about how to keep the body in top form. Point out that studies on aging demonstrate that body declines are largely attributable to inactivity, inadequate nutrition, and illness—all of which are largely within our control—rather than to the passing of years. You may feel especially grateful if you recall what many women looked and felt like only three decades ago, when they were told that aging was solely a matter of genetic inheritance.

If your daughter is nine or older, you may enjoy reading and discussing two books that explore the subject of eternal life: *Tuck Everlasting*, by Natalie Babbitt, and *The Merlin Effect*, by T. A. Barron. Books such as these can spark discussions that will allow you to share an important message: There is no fountain of youth. Aging gracefully and healthfully is what counts.

(12) Come to Terms with Any Envy You May Feel About Other Women's Bodies

How do you feel when you see a Victoria's Secret commercial featuring a long-legged, full-breasted model clad in skivvies? What about when you leaf through the pages of a fashion magazine or watch a favorite starlet on the big screen? If you feel a twinge of envy, you should know that you're not alone. Envy and the need to measure one's self against others has been with us since the dawn of humankind. In fact, we can use these occasional feelings of envy for the good if they encourage us to reach healthy and attainable goals. Unfortunately, in today's society, in which we are bombarded with one manipulated image after another and countless messages suggesting that we have to compete with everyone else—to be better looking, smarter, and more interesting—too many of us feel dissatisfied with our physical selves.

This is one implication that can be gleaned from the results of a survey conducted by an independent research firm for *People* magazine, in which one thousand women ages eighteen to fifty-five were polled. Thirty-seven percent of the respondents indicated that the portrayal of women on television and in the movies makes them feel insecure about their bodies. Twenty-four percent said they were bothered by images in fashion magazines, and 19 percent, by models used in advertising. One woman, a grandmother, explained that when she sees pictures of Julia Roberts, she tries not to look past her eyes because Roberts's figure makes her feel like a "slob."[2]

Another, more insidious and emotionally complex problem occurs when mothers envy their daughters. Since women can be so ashamed of these feelings that they keep them secret even from themselves, it's difficult to get them to own up to them. But some level of envy is to be expected. Many of us are giving our daughters the kind of lives we wish we had. Also, it's very human—in this youth culture—to compare ourselves unfavorably to our daughters, contrasting, for instance, our own skin that is beginning to wrinkle with our daughter's dewy complexion. And since human emotions are so complex, our reaction may also include, at the same moment, a surge of delight in her healthy glow. It can be a relief to acknowledge our darker, shadowy feelings.

When envy is repressed, some mothers attack their daughters' vulnerable body image. These attacks are sometimes delivered in the form of bitter criticisms: "Your hips are just so big." More passive approaches include envious "compliments," with a mother saying, for instance, "I would kill to have legs like yours." (A remark such as this could hardly allow a girl to take joy in her legs.) Another passive form of envy is comparisons, such as "You're lucky you don't have to worry about how much you eat. Everything I swallow shows on me."

When girls sense that their mothers are envious of any of their physical features, it makes them unnecessarily self-conscious and sometimes self-destructive. Michelle Joy Levine, Ph.D., a psychotherapist who has written about unconscious desires that contribute to obesity, takes this notion a bit further. She explains that an envied daughter feels under attack. Rather than further provoking her mother, she may become obese as a way of showing that she is not to be envied.[3]

If active envy has been a problem for you, do some journal writing about your own childhood experiences. Explore how envy affected relationships in your childhood home and whether you are acting out a family script. Envy is also connected to your level of self-esteem, which can be increased as you develop an appreciation for your own gifts.

(13) Understand Where Your Body Ends and Hers Begins

Although maintaining a strong parent-child connection is crucial in helping your daughter love herself, it's also possible to be too close to her. This situation occurs when a parent views a child as an extension of herself or himself, rather than as a separate and unique individual. Even when it's a well-meaning parent trying to give a daughter everything the parent never had—including a slim body—the child's life can be negatively impacted. One mother who had been overweight as a child took her twelve-year-old daughter to two different physicians, insisting that the girl was heading for obesity. Both physicians found the girl to be within the normal weight range for her height, but her mother put her on a diet anyway. When the girl began to resist her mother's controlling ways, the parents turned to a family psychologist for help. In therapy, the woman learned that in families in which there are control issues, parents often project onto offspring the image they had of themselves as children. Thus, this woman looked at her daughter and saw herself as a chubby adolescent. That's why she was having difficulty believing the physicians. In parent-child relationships with poor boundaries, overweight parents—in projecting their experiences onto their daughter—may unconsciously "set up" their daughters—by buying junk food and fast food, for instance. So their girls often grow up with the same body issues.

When parents don't wean their offspring from their control, children find it difficult to make independent and healthy choices concerning their bodies. In fact, a Pennsylvania State University researcher found that parents who try to keep overweight children from certain foods may prompt a variety of unhealthy behaviors, including overindulgence in non-nutritious foods, eating when not hungry, and avoidance of exercise.[4] In addition to food and weight, a parent may try to control a daughter's clothing, hair, and the activities in which she participates. In a battle to survive, an overly controlled adolescent may try to break the parental stranglehold in self-defeating ways, including under- or overeating. Psychotherapist Joy Levine believes that some overly controlled children overeat to exert their autonomy. She explains that expressing defiance in this way may be recognized and conscious or completely outside one's awareness. When overeating is an expression of defiance, it is as if the person is sticking out her tongue and chanting, "Na, na, na, na, na. I am eating all the foods I'm not supposed to eat and you can't do anything about it."[5]

If you have been trying to control most of what your daughter eats, you will find that the best time for changing your approach is after the two of you have had some time away from one another—perhaps after she returns from a summer camp, a school trip, etc. It will give you both the sense that you're starting out with a clean slate. You can tell your daughter that you have been too controlling, and that you want to support her in taking responsibility for her body.

Changing your approach will not be easy, but you should be aware that the need to control is always driven by fear. For this reason, you may want to explore the fears that may be keeping you (or her father) from allowing your daughter to control her own body. The following are a few suggestions:

· **Name your fears:** Ask your daughter to alert you when you're acting controlling. When she catches you at it, breathe deeply and figure out what happened to tap into your fears.

For instance, Donna's sixteen-year-old daughter is naturally slender, but Donna often urged her to eat calorie-rich foods. When Donna examined why her daughter's thinness frightened her, she discovered she didn't want people to think she was an inadequate mother who wasn't giving her child enough to eat. (This had been Donna's childhood experience.) Donna learned to back off when her daughter told her she'd had enough.

- **See yourself as a separate being:** On a large sheet of paper, draw two ovals about a foot high, making certain the edges of the two circles don't touch. Within one oval, record some of your opinions, interests, beliefs, preferences for clothing and entertainment, and other characteristics that make you unique from your daughter. In the second circle, fill in some details about your daughter.

  Now close your eyes and imagine these ovals floating off the page, as one surrounds you, and the other surrounds your daughter. See the two of you standing a few inches apart, each of you encased in a shimmering bubble that makes you a unique and separate individual. Do this exercise every time you feel yourself obsessing over the way your daughter looks. Remind yourself that when you criticize your daughter's efforts to make independent decisions concerning her body—complaining about her size is one good example—it's akin to using a needle to prick the "bubble" of well-being that surrounds her.

- **Write a letter to your daughter:** In a journal entry, tell your daughter about your attempts to mold her into the "perfect" individual that you felt you never were. Although this is for your eyes only, you should apologize (in person) for putting this burden on her.

- **Don't dictate what she'll wear:** Style of hair and clothing should be a matter of personal expression—remember how you used to look? Writing for *Time* magazine, Amy Dickinson recommends that mothers of young daughters gently guide their fashion choices by encouraging them to dress themselves and then praising their choices. Dickinson further recommends that when a girl age eight or nine chooses an inappropriate outfit, the parent should acknowledge her choice ("I can tell you think that's great!"), then compromise ("Let's just get the skirt today. I'm not sure that top is good for a kid your age").[6] If you're battling with your girl because she's wearing outfits you consider too provocative, get involved with the parents' board at your school and work at initiating or enforcing a school dress code.

· **Identify your own dreams:** Sometimes we hold on to our daughters because we're afraid that our own lives are empty. That's why we owe it to ourselves and to our children never to quit pursuing our own dreams. List your dreams and then circle the one that is closest to your heart. Set small goals, things you can do every day to move you closer to making your dream a reality.

Keep in mind that you can give your daughter emotional freedom only when you take responsibility for your own issues. You won't change your behavior overnight, but keep at it, and she'll be all the better for it.

(14) Model the Importance of Relaxing Your Body

Another area that is rife for change concerns the nonstop busyness of our lives. Some of us resemble the Eveready Bunny, for we keep going and going, and as a result are usually the last family members to rest. But at least the Eveready Bunny is cute; those of us who work until we drop simply look like workhorses, perhaps especially to our daughters. Watching us and knowing they'll eventually grow into women too, they may equate their future lives with thankless servitude. Our never-ending schedules may make them resentful of being born into feminine bodies.

If this is the case for you, and you want to raise a daughter who knows how to respect and love her body, it's crucial that you learn to slow down for a period each day and model relaxation. We know that taking time for yourself (and we mean regularly, not just during vacations) is a lot easier to say than do.

Even in two-parent families in which both adults work outside the home, many of us women are doing more than half the share of housework and child care. According to sociologist Arlie Hochschild, wives work about fifteen extra hours more each week than their spouses do. Over the course of a year, these hours add up to an extra month of twenty-four-hour days.[7] Single parents are obviously doing much more. And those of us who are stay-at-home-moms have also overloaded our schedules. Too many of us have been raised to believe that taking time for ourselves is selfish. Now it's time to change that message, for ourselves and for our girls.

It's important—even if you feel somewhat guilty—to announce to your daughter that you're going to start giving your body and mind time to relax. Then schedule times in your datebook or calendar, if necessary, and follow through. This schedule may mean, for instance, that one of your kids has to take a bus or ride a bike home one afternoon, rather than have you as the chauffeur. Respond to any objections by explaining that every body needs and deserves time out. These breaks can be as short as twenty minutes for meditation or journal writing, or longer if your schedule permits. Here are other suggestions for slowing down your body:

- Don't start a morning in which you may have unpleasant tasks ahead of you by telling your daughter that you wish the day were already over. Instead, model for her how, despite some inconveniences, you plan to enjoy being in your body by becoming more aware of your senses. That may

mean leaving home a little early for jury duty, parking far-
ther away than you planned, and walking the extra blocks as
you take time to *smell* the delicious scent emanating from
the bakery, *see* a colorful floral display, and *hear* the laughter
from a playground.

- Rather than fold clothes or do the laundry, take a midafter-
noon bath. You may hear your mother's voice in your head
preaching about the dangers of being an indolent woman, so
turn up your radio and enjoy yourself.

- The next time you're scribbling a note to your children or
mate, slow down and write it in your best penmanship. Note
the smooth interaction between your brain and fingers: you
think something and voilà! you're writing it down. Although
these notes take only minutes, they are a wonderful way to
say I love you—to the recipient of the note and to yourself.

- When you're racing to your next appointment, slow your
body down by recognizing the many functions that are
occurring right beneath your skin. For example, recognize
that you've just gone thirty seconds, the time your heart
needed to pump blood all the way through your body. And
you have good reason to believe that there will be many two-
week periods in your life for the growth of new taste buds
which will allow you to enjoy your favorite foods. Reflecting
on some of the tasks your body performs helps you recognize the abundance (rather than the scarcity) of time in your
life. You might feel moved to say, for instance, "Thank you,
God, for giving me enough time. I have more than enough
time." As the tension drains from your body, you can relax
even in the midst of an otherwise hectic schedule.

- Rushing in from a long day at work? Take a few minutes to
rest your mind and body by reading a selection from *I Am
Becoming the Woman I've Wanted,* an anthology of poems and
short writings edited by Sandra Haldeman Martz that won

the 1995 American Book Award. It will help you feel joyful for the naked truth of your body.

After a few weeks of learning to relax your body, encourage your daughter to follow suit. In addition to looking closely at her schedule and considering whether some activities need to be cut out to lower her stress level, find a time each day that she can allot to slowing down. Some girls tend to be very social and never develop the capacity to enjoy solitude. To them, sitting quietly or playing alone may seem too much like what an "unpopular" girl does with her time. That's unfortunate, because although being active can help our daughters to connect with their bodies, being still can give them time to "listen in" on their feelings.

You may want to start your daughter's relaxation training by cutting back on her schedule and fitting in relaxation times. Next, show your daughter a photo (if you have one) taken during a moment when she was enjoying her own good company. Perhaps she was entertaining herself at the beach or in her room, examining a leaf, staring out at the ocean, or stretched out on a hillside counting daisies. If so, have a copy of this photo made and give it to her to remind her of the contentment she is capable of experiencing.

If your daughter is ten or older, she may be more resistant to spending time on her own, but work with her on it. Suggest that she look through travel magazines with you to find a photograph of a place (not a person) on which she can focus. Tell her to imagine herself in that place. Of course, you won't want to force her to sit alone. Offer to snuggle with her, but insist that the two of you remain quiet. You can also try a synchronized breathing exercise. Simply sit so one of you has her head in the other's lap. The person who's stretched out can breathe normally while the other person matches her breaths. Try this exercise for five minutes, then switch positions and do it again.

(15) Give Her the Freedom Not to Smile

Babies catch on quickly that turning up the corners of their mouths is one of the best ways to get positive attention. And in a society in which women who don't smile are called bitches, we learn to keep smiling. In fact, one study found that women return smiles at a rate of 93 percent, compared to only 67 percent for men.[8] In many jobs traditionally occupied by women, employees are expected to remain gracious and smiling, no matter what they're feeling.

It's true that there are times when the social convention of smiling or looking pleasant is important. But after decades of propping up our cheeks to look cheerful at all times, we who have become mothers must consider the price our daughters can pay for disingenuous smiles. Nervous smiles communicate uncertainty, diffidence, or embarassment. A forced smile can look more like a grimace. And there will also be times in our daughters' lives when they will need to know how to show firmness and anger. If we have not taught them that they don't have to smile, they may find it difficult to convey their anger when they need to defend their bodies.

Beyond the importance of what our daughters can miscommunicate to others, there is the significance of the mind and body being in conflict when a girl feels her stomach churning and her mouth conveying good cheer. Girls who feel free to say, "I'm not smiling because I'm unhappy with . . . ," are not forced to use smiles like masks to trick others and themselves, hiding sorrow, confusion, or rage. We aren't suggesting that you teach your girl to stop smiling but, rather, that you teach her that she doesn't *have to* smile. This message will give her the self-confidence to project what she's genuinely feeling.

There are ways in which you can help your daughter with this issue. Catch her the next time she puts on a fake smile and say something along the lines of, "You probably don't feel much like smiling, do you?" When she's posing for a photograph, don't ask her to smile. Explain what emotional authenticity means by pointing to well-known women, such as Maya Angelou, the writer, performing artist, and educator, or Madeleine Albright, former secretary of state.

Whether sharing family stories or speaking as world leaders, both women have demonstrated a range of emotions. They aren't all smiles, nor are they all scowls. But when Angelou and Albright laugh we feel it so deeply that we can be joyful with them. When they are angry, we feel that a change is about to occur. Personifications of the term "a force to be reckoned with," Angelou and Albright remind us that when women project authentic emotions through their body language, they exude power, modeling a chance for our daughters to have real power in this world. Now that's something to smile about.

III

Dads
Fine-Tuning That Makes a Difference

By encouraging a balance of masculine and feminine aspects in their daughters' personalities, fathers are able to give their girls a sense of balance. And as a girl's first "boyfriend," a father can help his daughter feel comfortable with who she is as a girl and later as a woman. Your daughter will be a child for only a short time, but she can feel like daddy's girl for the rest of her life.

(16) Use Imaginative Play to Teach Her How Her Body Should Be Respected

There's something very special about a young girl playing an imaginative game with her father. It may be because for so much of their lives, fathers are trapped in the this-is-how-a-man-moves-through-the-world guise. Then suddenly, at play-time, the mask is removed, and there's daddy, looking oh-so-vulnerable in his love for his girl. One father may give life to a hand puppet and speak in a falsetto. Another may share his enthusiasm of toy trucks and G.I. Joes. No matter what games you create, keep in mind that with a little imagination, your next playtime can be a wonderful opportunity for you to show your daughter that her body should be treated respectfully.

There are a few rules for creating proactive playtimes. If your daughter wants you to join her in a game involving her doll-house you may want to suggest, for instance, that she get her dolls out in the yard for a game of jump rope or that the dolls begin their morning with some jumping jacks. If she wants to have a tea party for her teddy bears, perhaps one of the bears can ask for carrot sticks instead of cookies. If she's playing with G.I. Joe, perhaps one of the other figurines can offer Joe some pointers on how to carry a heavy backpack without injuring his back.

James, a college administrator in St. Louis, came up with an idea for a Ken and Barbie activity that he recalls with great fondness. Since James's girls often played with their Barbie dolls, he decided it was important for him to give voice and manner to his oldest girl's Ken doll. With him speaking for Ken, and his oldest daughter, Emma, playing Barbie, they enjoyed hours of tea parties, dances, and dates.

When James considered what he wanted to teach Emma about how she should eventually allow young men to treat her, he decided to make the Ken doll a real gentleman. "Ken" held doors for Barbie and seated her at the table. Most important of all, James felt that Ken should not make a big deal about Barbie's looks. Although he told her when he thought she looked especially pretty, he also praised her intelligence, creativity, and strong will. By the time Emma had outgrown Barbie, James's youngest girl, Robin, had taken her place.

Robin had a speech impairment and often used sign language to communicate. It never slowed down her playtime with Daddy, though. In fact, realizing how much her dad enjoyed chess, Robin suggested that they incorporate the pieces into their Ken and Barbie playtimes. Shortly afterward, James realized that Robin has an innate talent for the game.

All this occurred more than eight years ago, and Ken and Barbie have long since been packed away. Emma is away at college, and Robin—one of the top chess players in her national division—has overcome her speech impairment. When his daughters get serious about dating, James said he won't be overly concerned. His girls know exactly what kind of young man is good enough and how they should allow their bodies to be treated. Their dad showed them years ago, at the height of the tea party season.

(17) Acknowledge Her Physicality

Since your girl probably views you as being strong, you can help boost her image of herself as physically powerful by engaging with her in activities that you may normally reserve for a son. You might act as a wild bucking bronco and allow her to ride your back as she holds on with her strong arms and legs. You may want to engage her in a football game, teach her to climb a tree, or wrestle. When it comes to the latter, a lot of parents may hesitate over the idea of wrestling between a father and daughter. But if you think about it, you'll realize that this is the kind of play that teaches a girl that she can dictate what happens to her body, even when she's up against someone who's bigger and stronger.

There are additional benefits as well. According to psychologist Ross Parke, the author of *Fathers,* research indicates that children who have had a lot of physical stimulation, through play such as wrestling, actually get along better with their peers in nursery school. They do so because they have been given a better opportunity to regulate their social behavior. They've learned how to recognize and send emotional signals and to control those emotions when it's time to stop.[1] You don't have to take an expert's word for it. You can conduct your own research concerning how your girl responds. When she's wrestling with you, be sure to respond immediately to any commands she might give you, such as, "Stop!" or "I don't like that." You'll be reminded that in addition to having fun, she's learning how to set boundaries concerning her body.

For more ideas on helping your daughter to love all of who she is, check out the website www.dadsanddaughters.org.

(18) Teach Her to Read a Map

One of the best ways to raise a daughter who moves through the world with self-confidence is to teach her to read a map. Even today, surprisingly enough, many fathers teach their sons to read maps but assume that their daughters will have to ask others for directions. The underlying message, of course, is that anyone who has a female body and mind is too incompetent to make her own way.

What is more, educational researchers have suggested that there are significant cognitive differences that give boys better spatial skills than girls and that contribute to boys being better at reading maps.[2] But surely you want to challenge all lines of reasoning that may thwart your goal of raising a girl who feels peaceful in her feminine body and can take responsibility for her own life.

That's why you should hang a world map and another of your town or city on your daughter's wall and explain it to her. As she matures, she will enjoy having an illuminated globe as a nightlight. Encourage her to learn about the world through atlases, geography board games, and computer programs. During family car trips, encourage her to keep track of where you're traveling by finding the destination on a map. And when she's eight or older, buy her a compass, put it on a chain, and encourage her to wear it like a necklace. A compass may not be as attractive as a beaded choker, but it can certainly help her to get her priorities straight. And if you don't know how to read a map or point out the four directions yourself, learn how.

If your daughter is a teenager, rent the *Blair Witch Project* on video and watch it together. It's a scary movie, but it can eventually lead to a serious conversation about what it means to be on the right path in life. This is another way of stressing the importance of being true to one's self, independent of popular culture.

(19) Comb and Brush Her Hair

Since mothers often oversee tasks that include dressing and bathing their daughters, fathers seem especially to appreciate the intimacy involved in hair grooming. These times can also create some wonderful body memories for your girl. She will remember the feel of your hands shampooing, brushing, and styling her hair. One father recalls, "I loved it. It was time with her, and I got to show her that I took pride in her." This ritual allows a dad to convey love and admiration for one of his daughter's most cherished physical attributes.

According to Jungian analyst Virginia Beane Rutter, "Teaching your daughter to groom and care for her hair is a way to express love and respect for her femininity. Symbolically, it is also a way to honor her mind, her thoughts, her fantasies—all the cerebral activity, right brain and left brain, that is housed in her head." Rutter suggests that parents take time during hair care rituals to listen carefully to their daughters' thoughts and communicate respect for their intelligence.[3]

Hair care rituals are also excellent times for celebrating the uniqueness of your daughter's hair. If it's curly, you can ask her to shake her head so you can "hear bells ringing." If her hair is straight and heavy, you can describe it as "a curtain of silk." Hair that is coarse and super curly can be "so invigorating" that it "wakes up your fingers and makes them want to dance." Fine, silky hair can "put silkworms out of business." Whatever your daughter's hair may look or feel like, you have the power to help her feel that it is truly her crowning glory.

(20) Discuss Her Period with Her

When a girl's menstrual cycle begins, Dad is often left out of the conversation. Many girls insist that their fathers not be told, and some mothers make the mistake of going along with this demand. But unless the father is emotionally untrustworthy, this important time in your daughter's life should not be shrouded in secrecy. Menstrual collusion between a mother and daughter will lead your girl to believe that her period is something to be ashamed of. If your daughter is adamant about keeping silent, give her a little time to get accustomed to the idea and then have her mom explain that it would be unfair to leave you out of the conversation.

Once she has experienced maternal support following the onset of her period, your daughter will probably be more willing to let you discuss menstruation with her. You may want to find a private moment when you can introduce the subject by recalling your own adolescence and how it felt for you to undergo physical changes. You may have a funny story to tell about your voice cracking—something she may feel comfortable hearing about from you. You can invite her into the conversation by saying that since you know about puberty only from a boy's point of view, you're curious about how she's feeling about the changes she's experiencing. If she remains silent or offers only a few monosyllabic responses, that's OK, too. She doesn't have to talk, but it is important for her to know that she has her dad's as well as her mom's support in this step toward womanhood.

If possible, practice what you're going to say ahead of time. One father waited until his daughter was in her room with her stereo blasting, then pounded on her door. When the unsuspecting girl opened the door, her father spoke in a voice loud enough to be heard over the music—and certainly loud enough to be overheard in her younger brother's room. This dad shouted, "So, I hear you've got your period." His daughter slammed the door in his face. Only then did he realize that he had not chosen the best time or place.

(21) Don't Criticize Women's Bodies

In many cultures around the world, boys and men entertain themselves by observing feminine bodies and critiquing them. Perhaps you once engaged in this spectator sport, but have learned to tone down your comments now that you have a wife and daughter of your own. (Hopefully, if you were once a fan of *Playboy* or the *Sports Illustrated* swimsuit edition—or any publication featuring nude or semiclad women—you have disposed of your collection. If you haven't, you should.) Even if you are a father who is well attuned to your daughter's emotional needs, you may sometimes make the mistake of commenting on a woman's weight or size. When watching television, you might say, for instance, "Boy, is she a pig!" or "She's got shoulders like a linebacker."

It's not that women aren't also guilty of engaging in these cruel comments (as this is the way that insecure people try to reassure themselves that "at least" they look better), but these body-savaging comments are particularly harmful to your daughter when she hears them from you. Remember that her expectations about the way boys and men should view and interact with her come directly from what she observes from you. Your daughter could grow up and expect that men will view her with the same critical eye. In passing along this women-as-objects mentality, you will make your girl more anxious about her own physique. She may reason, "If Dad thinks that actress is a pig, he must think I look even worse."

Rather than focus on someone's size or shape, pay attention to characteristics that say something about who that person is, such as, "That older woman walks as if she's really happy with her body." Or, "Look at the ways she smiles with her eyes." If you hear your daughter criticizing others, rather than lecture her, challenge her to tell you something she liked about the person. One dad tried that with his daughter, who had commented that the new girl on the block had "ugly hair." When her father suggested that she "change her consciousness" by considering what she liked about the young woman, his daughter said, "I liked her skateboarder shoes." The girl's face brightened as she finished, "so maybe that means I'll finally have another girl in the neighborhood that likes to skateboard." When your daughter becomes less critical of others, her own inner judge will sound more affirming, thus allowing her to feel confident that others are not judging her harshly.

(22) Watch Those Teasing Words

Diane, a thirty-four-year-old jazz musician, recalls an incident that occurred more than three decades ago and made her aware of the discomfort she would long feel about her body. "Since my parents were separated and I lived with my mom, I was always excited when my father picked me up," she recalled. "So when I came out of my building and saw his car parked out front, I skipped to the curb. But instead of saying hello, my father said, 'Hey, bunny rabbit, you better stop hopping, 'cause you don't have nothing to shake, with your skinny self.' He began laughing, but I didn't join in. I felt like I was seeing myself through his eyes, and I understood why kids always compared me to the cartoon character Olive Oyl. I felt like a stick."

Diane's father didn't intend to be cruel, but he hurt her anyway. Many fathers use teasing as a way of communicating with their daughters. This kind of interaction can sometimes be fun for younger girls, but that's not necessarily the case for pubescent girls, who understandably feel acutely sensitive about their changing bodies.

Once good-natured teasing crosses the line, it becomes shaming behavior. Shame can make us feel that *we* are wrong and can create a sense of disassociation from the body, a flush followed by numbness. Shame is difficult for your daughter to avoid. We live in a society in which girls and women are set up to believe that they need to transform their looks to attain the ideal. Viewing themselves as flawed, girls and women accept the blame for not working out enough, not dieting more, not getting the right haircut, not finding the right lipstick or outfit.[4]

Shame can destroy self-confidence and can linger on because children internalize the parental shaming voice and continue to use it against themselves. Unlike other forms of shaming, teasing is a tricky problem because the perpetrator generally uses the I-was-only-joking defense, the implication being that the individual under assault is just "too sensitive" and therefore at fault. The truth is that some forms of teasing are angry, passive-aggressive behaviors that are somewhat like a wolf in sheep's clothing: It might look cute to others, but if you're the target, it bites. For that reason, teasing, especially by siblings and fathers, has been found to be a powerful influence on children who feel bad about their bodies.[5]

We aren't suggesting that you put an end to levity between you and your girl. But you can tell your daughter that you realize she's getting older and that you want her to tell you when you're beginning to cross a line. Also, consider whether teasing keeps you from having serious and meaningful conversations with your daughter. If so, here's a chance to create some real intimacy in your relationship. Tell your girl how you learned to interact with others through teasing, which can keep someone from disclosing authentic feelings. Invite her to tell you how she feels about what you've said.

If yours is a family in which put-downs are a problem, ask everyone to agree to a zero-tolerance policy. Some mild teasing is to be expected between siblings. But when it has reached a point where the target of this teasing often complains about it, it has gone too far. If this is the situation in your home, work with the members of your family to explore the roots of this cruelty. You need to assure your daughter that you're going to do your best to make your home a place where people can build on their self-confidence.

(23) Respect Her Pulling-Away-from-Daddy Phase

Forty-one-year-old Dennis, of Boston, has lived away from his ex-wife and kids for a decade but has remained close to his daughters, ages ten and fourteen. His ex-wife says her friends marvel that he is such a patient and loving father. But Dennis is disappointed about his relationship with his oldest daughter. Although he expected her to go through a cooling-off period toward him, "I wasn't prepared for her changed behavior. If I try to give her a hug, she acts like it's electroshock." He points out that this daughter seems perfectly comfortable sitting in her mom's lap. "Why does she hate me?" he asks. Dennis doesn't realize that his daughter's response to him is quite normal and healthy and that although her behavior may be hurtful, she is trying to come to terms with her new, more womanly body.

During adolescence, girls often begin to limit conversations with their fathers. When they do talk, the discussions usually revolve around practical information, current events, or social issues. In fact, Judith Kaufman, a psychologist who writes about issues involving girls, explains that during adolescence, the father-daughter relationship is often "lacking in intimacy, understanding, and acceptance."[6]

On the contrary, however, there are also many women who recall being closer to their fathers than to their mothers during adolescence and say they viewed their fathers as role models for how to succeed in the world. But even in these situations, boundaries in the relationships shift. Imagine that you're one of two neighbors living side by side amicably until the other neighbor decides, for whatever reasons, to build a fence around her land. The next time she sees you, she doesn't know how to say, "I still want us to be close; it's just that I had to build that fence, and, to tell the truth, it makes me feel better." That situation is not unlike what Dennis and his daughter experienced. In healthy families such as theirs, someone sends out clear signals, and people read them and behave accordingly.

In dysfunctional families, there are few boundaries. The "fence" never gets erected because the child doesn't feel that her dad will still love her if she separates. Despite her emerging sexuality, a daughter may put up with being uncomfortable when her dad touches her. It is not unusual for girls who are raised in these situations eventually to form relationships in which they continue to submit to unwelcome contact. A girl's relationship with her father is just that powerful, setting the stage for her future.

Dennis's daughter was serving notice that it was going to take her a while to get accustomed to her new body, so she needed him to back off a bit. Rather than knowing how to say it, she responded with loud screams if anyone (especially her dad) walked into her room without knocking and she rejected his hugs. Understandably, like most pubescent girls, she felt more comfortable around her mother.

Although a father may understand this cooling of affection, there's a good chance he will miss being treated like the special guy in his daughter's life. Still, the father's response to his daughter's pulling away also serves as a model. If he signals that he still loves her and respects her body, despite her new boundaries, then he's preparing her to seek future relationships in which her body and her feelings are honored.

The best way for you to signal your acceptance of her new body is to ask permission for a hug or a kiss. This way, in a few years, your daughter will walk in the door, back from camp, college, or perhaps a tour abroad, throw her arms around your neck, and greet you with affectionate hugs. You will know that her renewed body comfort is a reward for having handled this situation with sensitivity.

IV

Parents Together or Apart
Speaking in One Voice About Body Esteem

Sometimes parents occupy the same house but in their busyness they rarely engage in long and meaningful conversations. Other parents live apart because of relationship difficulties. One thing they can usually agree upon is that they want the best for their daughters. Whatever your circumstances, there are certain behaviors that both of you should encourage in your girl if you hope to send her out into the world feeling that she stands on solid ground. You'll both know you're getting it right if she eventually looks at you with impatience and says, "Mom [or Dad] tells me the same thing."

(24) Show Up

Although your life may not be at a point at which you can attend all your daughter's games or performances, work toward that goal. Even if your daughter is at an age when she tells you that it doesn't matter if you show up for her events, remember that it does. We'll leave it to you as to how you'll manage, shifting vacation schedules or swapping chores with a friend or neighbor. If there's a tournament or other major event that you can't make, ask the team manager to take photos or video, so you can discuss the highlights with your girl later. And whenever she returns home from a game that you've missed, ask her to demonstrate for you how she moved or what she did. What does you seeing her have to do with her loving her body? The answer seems easier to discern if you consider the experiences of younger girls.

Sometimes it seems that no matter what you're doing—inching your way along a winding highway with a carload of youngsters or deep in thought, calculating what you will owe on your income taxes—your daughter's voice interrupts your concentration. "Look at me!" Though you may have warned her not to distract you, she always seems to forget. To rephrase Descartes' famous saying, "I think, therefore I am," for our children, the operative phrase is, "Mommy [or Daddy] sees me, therefore I am." In fact, it's so important for her to be acknowledged by you that she's willing to risk your displeasure to get your attention.

This should not be surprising. In a world that seems so large and complex, a child who depends on you for survival wants to know that you *see* her as a presence. In fact, your daughter can internalize a vision of how she fits into the world through a process called "mirroring," as you positively reflect who she is.

What we mirror to our children has a powerful influence on the way our children see themselves. Psychotherapist Michelle Joy Levine, Ph.D., explains that when a parent mirrors back to a child that she is lovable, good, smart, and pretty and that the parent is enthusiastically interested in her, the child internalizes these thoughts about herself.[1]

When a girl is young, mirroring may be as simple as giving her a round of applause the first time she successfully recites the alphabet or stooping down to get eye-level with her when she speaks. When she grows older, as she competes or performs in the larger world, your presence helps to convey your admiration and approval. Looking out into the audience or crowd, whether seeing you or sensing your presence, she will feel that you accept her and are proud of who she truly is and how she looks, rather than a fantasy of who she is.[2] When her activity has ended, give her specific feedback about what you saw. Rather than say, "good job," for instance, you might say, "That was a great jump shot during the fourth quarter."

Perhaps you'd imagined that by the time she becomes a teenager, her powerful need for her parents will disappear. After all, you have to wonder, if she cares about you seeing her, why does she act so hostile? It's one of many mixed messages of adolescence. Your daughter may push you away, but she doesn't actually want you to leave. If there is a secret here, it's not that she wants to post "keep out" signs on her door and, indeed, on her very life, but that your presence at her public events allows her to feel rooted. Through your eyes and heart, you place her in the world.

And so it is that at the chess championship, musical, volleyball finals, science fair, school debate, spelling bee, Girl Scout dinner, or violin concert, she wants your tributes, even those that are silent to everyone else's ears. By showing up, you are conveying, "You are a presence that counts in this world, and I love seeing you." Since your daughter will learn to view herself much as you do, your steady presence at her activities means she will learn to love seeing herself, too.

(25) Teach Her to Make Eye Contact

Long before your daughter could speak or even understand your words, the two of you used your eyes to communicate with each other. Psychiatrist Daniel Stern believes that the most basic lessons of emotional life are taught during these intimate eye-to-eye communications, when a parent conveys to a child that her emotions are met with empathy and that they are accepted and reciprocated.[3]

With this eye communication in mind, you can explain to your daughter that her eyes can be quite powerful and that when used correctly, they can convey silent and powerful messages to other people. Explain that one reason this gesture is so powerful is that although making eye contact is one way of communicating respect and empathy, few young people actually use it outside the home. Taught to be wary of strangers, they often avoid direct gazes. When they become teenagers, they generally limit eye contact, except, of course, when they're flirting.

You can show your daughter how to use her eyes like a strategic missile system—narrowing them and shooting sparks of anger if she needs to protect her personal space. Telling someone to get lost without opening your mouth is a powerful statement. Explain that averting her eyes also sends a message and should be used sparingly, for people both young and old tend to distrust those who avoid eye contact.

Tell her that, on the other hand, making eye contact is one of the most special body communications of all because it's a way of signaling interest. Demonstrate for her how to make eye contact when greeting a friend or teacher or someone's parents. Point out people you might notice who know how to use their eyes effectively.

(26) Don't Argue About Her Size

The family was enjoying one of their rare, unhurried breakfasts together. But as soon as their ten-year-old daughter left for school, Judy's husband, Darryl, demanded to know why she allowed their daughter to eat so much. This wasn't the first time Darryl had blown up about their daughter being chubby. His wife responded as she always did during these arguments: "She's a big girl, like me. If you don't like the way she looks, talk to her about it." Both parents left for work feeling defeated.

Darryl and Judy are like so many parents who argue over their daughter's body. They focus on their children to distract them from the pain in their own relationship, seldom realizing how much pain they're leaving in their wake. Although Darryl and Judy waited until their daughter left before they argued, on some level their girl was aware of this conflict.

Children tend to blame themselves for not being able magically to keep their parents at peace. When there is conflict between parents—silent or acknowledged, direct or indirect—children see themselves as flawed. In Darryl and Judy's home, his complaining about their daughter was his way of getting back at his wife, who had become obese.

Another father in a similar situation never complained about his overweight daughter, but spent a great deal of his time away from home engaged in extensive workout routines. When he was home, he pointedly refused desserts, saying: "I don't want to get fat." His unspoken words seemed to echo through the dining room: "fat like you." Although everyone in the family pretended to ignore his painful words, they felt them nevertheless. His daughter recalled, "I always felt daddy was looking right at me when he talked about being fat. Now Mom says he was really talking to her." There are many ways in which these parental weight conflicts are acted out. Here are a few examples:

· **A parent shields an obese child from a thin spouse:** In this scenario, an overweight parent defends the overweight daughter by suggesting that the other parent is making "too big a deal" of the girl's weight. Feeling shut out, the thin parent intensifies workout routines. Torn between her warring parents, the girl continues to overeat to soothe herself.

- **A child sides with one warring parent and signals disapproval of the other with her weight:** After her parents' divorce, a girl reasons that her father, who used to complain about his wife being overweight, will not love her unless she's thin. She shows she's different from her mother by starving herself.

- **Both parents obsess over thinness and the child acts out with food:** The parents distract themselves from their loveless marriage by obsessing over their own weight-loss diets. Feeling abandoned and unloved, the daughter acts out her anger by becoming obese, then later becomes bulemic.

- **The child becomes the family status symbol:** The parents distract themselves from their unhappiness by focusing on status symbols, such as a luxurious home and car. And in a world in which many people believe you can't be too rich or too thin, they also look to their slender daughter to increase their social status. Fearing that her parents will emotionally abandon her if she doesn't keep up appearances, the girl exercises and diets obsessively.

The only way out of these undeclared wars is an improved parental relationship. Fortunately for Darryl and Judy, they consulted a family therapist. In therapy, when Darryl admitted that he was resentful about his wife's weight, she opened up about her anger with him for "never being home" and admitted that she overate to get back at him. Their therapeutic work was challenging, but it helped take the pressure off their daughter.

That spring, Darryl bought bicycles for his wife and daughter and made time to join them for bicycle outings. The family eventually took a bike trip through Europe, and they have competed as a family in charity bikeathons. We're intentionally not going to tell you whether their daughter, or Judy, for that matter, slimmed down. The goal in healthy families is fitness, not slimness. We will tell you that their girl is learning to be comfortable in her body. If you work at healing your marital issues and at keeping concerns about your daughter's body out of the middle of your relationship, you will make it easier for her to see her body as her own.

(27) Compete with Boy Craziness

When you hear the term "boy crazy" you may remember it from your own childhood and view it as harmless and somewhat old-fashioned. But if you hope to cultivate an appreciation of your daughter's looks independent of the opinions of her peers and popular culture, you'd be making a mistake to confuse today's brand of boy mania with the crushes of yesteryear. Bolstered by the media, this millennial version of boy craziness can definitely affect a girl's relationship with her body as she submits to loud messages that dictate how she should look and behave.

Today's boy craziness starts as young as age seven and can survive into adulthood, even influencing a young woman's decision about where to attend college and, later, where she will move for her career. But long before high school and college, boy craziness can affect relationships between girls, dominating their conversations and thus taking attention away from a wider range of interests. One girl may volunteer, "I'll fix your hair so that new boy in class will notice you." Or an athlete may say, "I have to score a lot of points in this basketball game because Eric will be watching." After a while, not much else seems to matter but pleasing boys, and soon friends with richer interests are driven away. Some girls may initially pretend to be boy crazy—it's an easy and safe way to win or retain friends—and eventually start to believe their own words. In many school cultures, it's safer to be boy crazy because girls who are not are branded as "losers" and are shut out from popular groups.

The media certainly promote that view, with successful shows such as television's *Felicity,* a drama in which the main character planned to attend Stanford University and later, medical school. Instead she moves to New York to pursue a boy who has written in her yearbook that he wished he could have known her better. Though the premiere of the show was covered extensively by major news organizations, there was little, if any, criticism of its unhealthy message for girls. Several other teen-oriented shows, including *Dawson's Creek,* espouse a get-him-at-any-cost gospel. This message is underscored by a plethora of highly popular teen magazines that offer a steady diet of information about how girls can win the boys of their dreams. In 2000, one popular teen magazine, for instance, included an article entitled "Go-for-It-Girls Who Saw Boys They Liked and Went After Them." The article included a list of dos and don'ts for "snag-proof hook-up hints."

You don't have to read publications or tune in to a teen show to learn about boy craziness. One woman in St. Paul, Minnesota, told us that while returning from his first day of middle school, her twelve-year-old boy was chased by a "pack" of frenzied girls who wanted to be the first to claim him. Another mother, in the upscale town of Atherton, California, said a girl called her fifth-grade son every five minutes for a half hour until the boy agreed to speak to her. The girl invited him out on a date. The boy declined. Most surprising of all, perhaps, was that her phone campaign had been encouraged by her mom who believes that girls are usually too passive.

The subjects of this frenzy, the boys themselves, often have a different stance. They reach puberty two or three years later than girls, and when they do, they are likely to retain a greater sense of self. Few boys view girls as a way to self-define. Also, the amount of time devoted to the pursuit of girls differs. Although many adolescent boys care about dressing, talking, and acting cool so they can attract girls, rare is the young man who devotes hours, including long discussions with his friends, to his body, clothing, and hair so girls will deem him physically acceptable.

Unfortunately, this is standard behavior for many girls. The how-to-interest-the-guys formula requires girls to invest enormous amounts of time, energy, and money on dieting, makeup, and clothes so they can look a certain way to attract the boys. Girls who do not live up to the "popular girl" image are often made to feel physically flawed by their peers. But it's also a no-win situation for popular girls. Many come to believe that all they have to offer is their looks, and they may lose any sense of their uniqueness. For some children, boy craziness can also mean early and inappropriate sex, putting them at risk of pregnancy and sexually transmitted diseases.

There are indications that as early as the eighth grade young people—wealthy as well as impoverished—are engaging in oral sex and mutual masturbation. And while there are no in-depth studies available to indicate how many young people are participating in oral sex exclusively, at least one expert has noted a gender trend. Deborah Tolman, a director at the Wellesley College Center for Research on Women, told the *New York Times* that based on anecdotal information she has received, when it comes to oral sex, "the boys are getting it, the girls, no."[4] Obviously, not all boy-crazy girls participate in such self-defeating behavior, but we do urge you to take notice and prepare a defense. There's no way you can eradicate boy craziness, but you can compete with it. Here's how:

· **Keep the parental connection intact:** Girls who feel emotionally abandoned by one or both parents are more likely to desperately seek attention from boys. Because adolescence can be a time of rebellion and distancing, many parents pull away from their daughters, completely losing the connection. But if your daughter has to look to boys to feel love and admiration, important boundaries may be crossed.

- **Help her discover her own needs:** If you walk into your daughter's room and find that she has turned it into a shrine to boy celebrities, ask her to point out her favorite guy, and find out what she admires about him. Ask what kind of boy she needs to make her happy. Then ask her to tell you what the right boy would find positive about her. If she begins by listing physical features, steer her toward her many other attributes.

- **Use that energy:** If your daughter feels she needs more money to pay for a certain style that is deemed necessary for popular girls, view it as an opportunity to hone her uniqueness. Encourage her to start her own business, for instance, selling her handmade jewelry at a flea market. This will require her to use her math skills so she can record her business transactions, including investments, profits, and expenditures.

- **Consider incentives:** If your daughter is desperate to see or hear one of her favorite boy groups, promises of concert tickets (or new CDs) can serve as wonderful enticements for improved grades, completed chores, or read-a-book-a-week summers.

(28) Encourage Her to Develop a Special Talent

Every one of us has a special talent, and developing this gift gives us a chance to connect with the inner spirit. Throughout various religious traditions, the Divine is often referred to as the "Creator." It is this life force within that is expressed in great works of art, as well as in everyday creations.

Girls who are given opportunities to identify and develop their special talents will find it easier to negotiate the awkwardness of adolescence and present themselves to the world with more confidence. Passion for a creative endeavor can also take the focus off the body and allow girls to feel more at peace with themselves. Playing the cello, harp, or violin, for instance, can help a girl feel regal. A shy girl may find that playing the drums puts her in touch with an untapped ferocity. Or a girl with a learning disability, who gets teased by others because of her poor reading skills, may feel more confident after hearing her artwork praised.

That's what happened with Patricia Polacco, who as an adult became an award-winning author and illustrator of children's books, including *Thundercake* and *Chicken Sunday*. Polacco is dyslexic, and even as an adult, struggles with reading. As a child, she developed more self-confidence when her mother had some of her artwork framed and invited friends, family, and neighbors to their Oakland, California, home for art shows. Their compliments and serious treatment of her work helped Polacco start to see herself as gifted.

A special talent doesn't necessarily have to involve the arts, of course. A girl may enjoy designing computer programs, special gift wraps, or greeting cards, or excel at candle- or soap making, wood carving, photography, quilting, pottery, knitting, embroidery, or gardening. What's important is that you not assert your will. Your daughter should be allowed room to discover on her own where her talents lie. It is the unknown, or the Great Creator within each of us, that gives birth to a thought that may be transformed into a brush stroke, musical composition, quilt, or garden. One book series that will inspire your daughter to be more creative is *Portraits of Women Artists for Children*, by Robyn Montana Turner, which celebrates the lives and works of notable artists.

(29) Give Her a "Body" of Knowledge

If ever there was a way to help your daughter confidently present herself to the world, teaching her to love to read ranks right up at the top. Reading is like a workout for the brain: scientists have discovered that regularly stimulated channels of activity literally create and reinforce new neural connections. Reading is also a window to the world and can bolster your daughter's confidence in the way she communicates and presents herself. You may already have a daughter who loves to read, and to you we say, Bravo! But if your daughter spends hours on-line or on the telephone or is glued to the television, it's not too late to help her develop a lifelong love affair with books.

If she's eight or under, you're probably still reading to her every night. And that's great because there is simply no other bedtime ritual more loving than curling up together and bringing the world up close by turning the pages of a book. When children grow older, however, generally around the fourth or fifth grade, parents often stop reading with their children and encourage them to read independently. Not only do they spend less time together, but for some children, the joy of reading is diminished. That doesn't have to be the case. In addition to modeling for her the importance of reading when she sees you read and hears you talking about books, there is much you can do. The following are some suggestions for giving your daughter a body of knowledge:

- **Stress the magic:** Rather than tell her that she should read so she will be more successful, stress the point that reading is magical. And it is. It enables humans to look at symbols on a page and be transported to distant places.

- **Create school "reading zones":** Persuade administrators at your daughter's school to hold a "Reading Zone Day." During these hours, a banner is hung outside the school that reads "Sssh! This Is a Reading Zone." The entire school is hushed as everyone reads, from the principal to teachers, to maintenance workers. Children can wear pajamas and slippers and can bring along pillows and stuffed animals.

- **Let her sleep on it:** Set bedtimes a half hour early and tell your daughter that the lights can remain on as long as she is reading. After a long day, chances are she will fall asleep after only a few minutes, but this is a great way to drift off.

- **Give her "time out" from reading:** When your daughter misbehaves, tell her she is not allowed to read. This will give her the impression that reading is a privilege and something to be treasured and savored, which it is.

- **Read the book, rent the video:** Choose a great book that has been made into a film, and after taking turns reading the book aloud (or separately), rent the video, then compare the book and movie. The Ann of Green Gables series is an excellent choice, because the book focuses on a heroine who doesn't have conventional beauty but who is indeed beautiful in spirit. *Little Women,* by Louisa May Alcott, is another great selection, because it stresses the value of character over exterior trappings.

- **Share Assigned Readings:** When your daughter is old enough to get assigned reading lists from school, pick out a few of your favorites and ask her to read portions aloud to you. Your enthusiasm for the literature will help your daughter view classics, such as *Treasure Island,* as the gems they truly are.

- **Remember audio books:** These are especially fun on family car trips. Also, books on tape can be helpful if your daughter is diagnosed with a learning disability. That way, while she is learning the mechanics of reading, she doesn't get turned off to books. Once she's more secure in her reading skills, she will switch over to books in print. One of the best juvenile books on tape (for children age ten and over) is *The Giver,* by Lois Lowery.

- **Family book outings:** Get your family together on a Friday or Saturday evening for a quick dinner and then an outing to a bookstore. You can spend the evening browsing through favorite sections and thumbing through stacks of books.

- **Support your local library:** Don't let your daughter take public libraries for granted; they are one of the greatest gifts of our society. In addition to taking your daughter on regular visits and consulting with the librarian for book selections, donate books and money to your closest branch. And if your local libraries are closed on Sundays, start a campaign to change their schedules.

- **Have regular family reading nights:** With the television off, computers shut down, and phone calls ignored, read aloud the Harry Potter series (which features a girl character—Hermione Granger—who is smart and full of common sense). For independent reading, when family members gather but individuals read silently from their own selections, pick up a copy of *Great Books for Girls,* which includes more than 600 suggestions by Kathleen Odean, a librarian and member of the prestigious Caldecott and Newberry Award committees. Girls ages twelve and up may also enjoy *Stargirl,* by Jerry Spinelli, about a high school girl who holds on to her true identity.

- **Urge her to read more than books:** Share newspaper stories about other children, in her country as well as abroad. When playing family games, designate her (and any other siblings) as the official readers of instructions.

- **Promote bathroom reading:** Place a book-magazine rack in your bathroom. Though critics may label this practice déclassé, what's important is promoting literacy. Be sure to stock some children's anatomy books in this bathroom rack.

- **Join a mother/daughter or father/daughter book club:** These book clubs are wonderful fun, whether gathering with two or more duos and meeting once a week or monthly. For more information on launching one of your own, pick up a copy of *Mother/Daughter Book Club,* by Shireen Dodson and Teresa Barker. One excellent true-life adventure story that can be shared by a father and his teenage daughter is *Two for* *the Summit: My Daughter, the Mountains, and Me,* by Geoffrey Norman.

(30) Assign Chores and Follow Through on Enforcing Them

For busy parents, assigning chores and making sure our children actually do them is a real, well, chore. Although we don't doubt the importance of chores, many of us are reluctant to add them to our daughters' busy schedules. Let kids be kids, right? Well, in fact, it probably isn't right. This attitude can hit your daughter where it hurts: in her body. A child without limits—who feels, for example, that she can leave anything where she drops it and defy expectations without consequences—will have difficulty feeling confident about becoming an independent being. Though the connection seems indirect, chores are part of boundary setting and responsibility taking. In this respect, they contribute to your daughter's taking responsibility for her body.

It's true that this will require a time commitment from you, but good parenting is time-consuming, and we do need to create situations in which our daughters experience the consequences of their actions. Consequences can help your daughter feel confident about managing her body and her life. The idea is to begin small and then branch out to more complex chores. Here are some tips on chores and healthy follow-through:

- **List chores:** Call a family meeting, and after everyone enjoys a meal and a chat, announce that you're putting together a list of chores and ask for suggestions. These chores can include emptying the dishwasher, changing the kitty litter, sweeping the front steps, and so forth. Allow your children to choose one chore; they can eventually work up to more.

- **Discuss natural consequences:** Explain to your children that you won't chase them around to get the work done, but you will check later, so they'll have to perform their chores or experience consequences. This does not mean vengeful or arbitrary punishment, such as not going to the prom or having their CD collection taken away. "Natural" means the consequence is tied to the misbehavior. For instance, if your daughter has to empty the dirty the clothes hampers on Saturdays, the day the laundry is done, and ignores her obligation, she is throwing off the laundry schedule. Consequences may include having to do her own laundry or paying to have the clothes washed at an outside laundromat.

- **Do advance work:** Try to figure out a logical consequence in advance, but if you are caught by surprise, simply say, "There will be consequences for this" and then give yourself time to think, rather than hurl some unenforceable threat at her.

- **Remain firm:** When the time comes for her to perform her chore, there should be no nagging or reminding. You will have to be firm as well as loving. If your daughter is rushing off to school and doesn't have clean clothes, you may simply say, "I'm sorry, but since you didn't bring your clothing downstairs, you'll have to make do for this week." It's important to let her know that she will have a chance to redeem herself the following week. Be prepared for your daughter to beg or harass you, but remain firm and don't get pulled into her drama; simply refer to the agreement that you have. Keep your side of the conversation to a minimum.

- **Consider charging for uncompleted tasks:** Explain to your children that they may be billed for not completing chores that could interfere with normal family functioning, such as cleaning up the kitchen so you can prepare dinner when you return home. Perhaps a dirty kitchen means that you have to order sushi from a local restaurant and your daughter will have to pay for it. If necessary, present your child with a bill, and insist that she pay you.

- **Don't forget praise:** Let her know when she has done a good job with her chore. But don't go overboard; a few words of acknowledgment will suffice.

- **Learn more about setting limits:** You may want to participate in a program called STEP, which stands for Systematic
  Training for Effective Parenting. For more information,
  write to STEP Coordinator, American Guidance Service,
  Publishers' Building, Circle Pines, MN 55014-1796.

(31) Support Teens in Getting Summer Jobs

In a world in which so much emphasis is placed on how women
look, the summer-job experience offers teenagers opportunities
to see themselves as strong and capable beings. Unfortunately,
many parents are giving money to their children, rather than
encouraging them to work to help defray college costs or to
earn spending money. Since 1990, fewer teenagers and young
adults have been joining the summer workforce. In 1999, just
62 percent of America's 16 million young people ages sixteen to
nineteen were in the labor force, compared with a high of 71.8
percent in 1978. This is the lowest percentage of summer youth
employment since 1965.[5]

Our daughters may be the biggest losers in this summer
employment trend. It's important for them to grow up believing that no matter what, they can feed and clothe and provide
shelter for themselves and that eventually they won't have to
depend on someone else to do it for them. And in a society in
which money talks, earning your own can give you a voice.
Besides, cashing a paycheck with your name on it can help you
stand taller.

If your daughter resists summer work, compromise with her
and create a plan that allows her to work part of her summer
vacation, while leaving time to pursue other interests. No, she
might not thank you for insisting. But need we remind you
that this is one more reason that children have parents, rather
than friends, to raise them?

(32) Encourage Her to Participate in Sports

Athletics are a celebration of the human form, and since the passage of Title IX, the landmark 1972 law that requires schools to give equal opportunities to both sexes in sports programs, our girls have jumped at the chance to participate. As a result, the number of girls playing high school varsity sports has increased by more than 500 percent. Despite these growing numbers, Colette Dowling, the author of *The Frailty Myth*, explains, parents tend to enroll their girls in sports activities two years later than they do boys who participate in sports. "That means they're behind from the get go in learning the skills needed for physical competence. This disadvantage . . . is enough to dissuade many girls from trying further. Seventy percent of children reject organized sports before the age of thirteen, but the fallout rate of girls is six times that of boys."[6]

This situation is unfortunate because athleticism can boost a girl's confidence in what she can accomplish with her body and help her understand how her body can learn to do something it couldn't do before. And because the focus on sports requires participants to view their bodies as functional rather than decorative, female athletes can develop an unwavering sense of their physical competence. This is crucial, explains Dowling: "A belief in the competence of one's body is essential—for mental health, for physical safety, for fulfillment in relationships and success in the workplace."[7]

Much of the emphasis in sports is placed on physical endurance, but if you find yourself questioning whether sports are right for your daughter, remember that athleticism has a spiritual side. Strength and agility are important, but so is calm self-assurance and emotional and physical self-mastery in the face of extreme pressure. Runners, tennis players, boxers, and others who are involved in one-on-one competitions must be intensely self-aware. Forced to confront their deepest fears, a player may ask, "Why am I holding myself back?" or "What must I do to reach my next goal?"

When we asked a few girls to explain how their involvement in sports affects their relationships with their bodies, here's what they said:

"My brain tells me to lunge for that tennis ball, and my body obeys. Whoa! That feels good."

"You start relying on your body, so you know you have to take care of it."

"Sports make me grateful for my body. In the middle of a basketball game, the crowd around me blurs, I hear footsteps behind me, sense movement to my left, race across the floor with my eye tight on the ball."

Above all, encourage your daughter to participate in a sport for the sheer enjoyment of it, not necessarily because she'll be the best on the team. She may also decide to get involved because she likes the exercise or being part of a team effort. No matter what motivates her, experiencing the physical self in action is a clear step toward body esteem.

V

Body Armor

Saving Her Body from the Assault of Popular Culture

For a long time, many of us have been stymied about how we can protect our daughters from "being tyrannized by the images of popular culture."* Most of us don't want to isolate our girls, and yet we have become increasingly aware of societal messages that suggest that the female body exists purely for the entertainment and profit of others. Well, we don't have to take it anymore. We can teach our daughters how to view their bodies lovingly in the face of enormous pressure.

*This phrase is from an essay by Ann Taylor Fleming, on *The NewsHour with Jim Lehrer*, PBS, June 20, 2000.

(33) Strengthen Her Against the Power of Advertising

The fairy tale "The Emperor and His New Clothes" can be read to young girls as a way of protecting them from the advertising barrage that attempts to dictate what their bodies are supposed to look like, how they should dress, and even what they should smell like. This is an opportunity to help your daughter avoid taking popular standards too seriously and resist the grip that advertisers have on our psyches. This is not a subject to be taken lightly. Advertising has the power to make your daughter feel uncomfortable in her own skin, generating self-criticism, anxieties, and doubts. Advertising is such a powerful influence because it normalizes unhealthy body behaviors. For instance, television commercials have convinced millions of people that it is normal and healthy to regularly polish off fast food meals and, later, to drink diet supplements to help reduce body fat. With our help, our daughters can see advertising in a new light.

Explain to your daughter that like the tailors who sold the emperor his invisible clothing, advertisers will say practically anything to convince people to buy their goods: clothing, shoes, makeup, and hair, skin, and dental preparations, as well as foods and other products. Show your daughter illustrations in the "Emperor" story, and point out how proud and superior the emperor felt when he thought he was wearing his grand clothing.

Tell her that like the tailors, people who create commercials try to convince us that a product can also make us feel a certain way. For instance, shampoo commercials don't simply promise clean hair. They also suggest that once we use a particular shampoo, we'll become the life of the party. Ask your daughter if she wants to be like the people on the road who cheer the emperor when he strolls by naked, or whether she would like to be the wise child who speaks the truth.

Your daughter will need to know that there's nothing wrong with wanting to feel pride or acceptance. The problem with some commercials is that they can be deceptive. A new pair of expensive sneakers may make her feel proud for a short while, but the pride of ownership pales next to what she may feel if she practices running the mile and learns to use her feet and legs and spirit to keep going even when she gets tired.

If your daughter is thirteen or older, she may enjoy learning that advertisers create commercials that appeal to consumers on a subconscious level. Explain that these companies hire psychologists who have spent years studying the human mind. They understand what makes us feel superior or inferior or fearful or envious and then use this information to try to convince us that we can feel a certain way if we buy their products. She may enjoy analyzing some commercials by considering what the advertisers were trying to make her feel and whether they succeeded.

Older girls may also enjoy reading and discussing "The Necklace," a powerful story by Guy de Maupassant, who writes of a woman whose life is destroyed by her desire for expensive clothing and jewels.

Finally, you can suggest to your girl that the next time she sees a commercial that tells her what her body is supposed to look like, she should remind herself that she's already fine just the way she is. Angela, the mother of six-year-old Tracy, worried when she explained this concept that Tracy was too young to understand. But the next time the television was turned on and Tracy saw a shampoo commercial, she shook her fist at the set and yelled, "You're not the boss of me." We say Amen to that.

(34) Explain That Those Xtremely Cool Soda Ads Mask a Threat to Her Skeletal System

Soft drink companies have been targeting increasingly younger consumers with a barrage of commercials and product placements that make drinking sodas appear cool. Many young people now view soft drinks as the stuff of life. Since 1978, there has been a threefold increase of soda intake among teenagers and double the intake for children ages six to eleven.[1]

With images of trick bikers, skateboarders, and volleyball players, the young actors in soft drink commercials may look cool, but remind your daughter of what those advertisements *aren't* saying—that soft drinks can pose a major threat to her skeletal system. Researchers at the Harvard School of Public Health have found that active girls who regularly drink soda are five times more likely than nonsoda drinkers to have bone fractures.[2] One explanation for this difference may be that in addition to drinking less water and fruit juice, many children who chug sodas drink less milk—a significant source of calcium and vitamin D in the American diet. Studies indicate that many girls do not consume enough calcium to build strong bones.[3]

A lot of children are also consuming the equivalent of three to five cups of coffee a day in caffeinated sodas.[4] You probably already know that caffeine can cause anxiety and sleeplessness. Fewer people seem aware that colas—the leading soft drinks—contain phosphorus, which can impede the body's ability to utilize dietary calcium when calcium intake is low.[5] Compounding the insult to the body, caffeine is a diuretic, which can cause dehydration. Colas can also discolor teeth, robbing them of their luster.

With all this bad news, you have to wonder why so many of us continue to buy soda, the best selling of all grocery products. The truth is that many of us keep buying soda for our children despite its ill effects because many of us drink it ourselves and don't want to give it up.

The only solution is for everyone in the family to cut back on soda. And educate your daughter about the drawbacks of what she may be drinking. Each time we explain the connection between bone fractures and caffeinated soft drinks most active girls say it isn't worth the risk. One volleyball player grew wide-eyed as she considered whether there was a connection between her regimen of three diet colas a day and the pain she had suffered from numerous breaks and fractures, as well as time lost on the sidelines.

Also, educate your daughter about the caffeine breakdown of her favorite soft drinks. For example, the average eight-ounce cup of Starbucks coffee contains about 190 milligrams of caffeine, while a supersized caffeinated drink is the equivalent of three cups of coffee. A can of Coca-Cola has 45 milligrams of caffeine, and Pepsi, 37. Two popular soft drinks that would seem to be caffeine free, Mountain Dew and Sunkist, actually have 55 and 40 milligrams of caffeine respectively.[6] You can also eliminate sodas from your shopping list and replace them with healthier choices, such as water and sparkling fruit juices.

Away from home, there is much you can do to get support from other parents. Make your views known at the beginning of each sports season and suggest a policy of no soda, and juice instead, for after-game refreshments. Parent power can also be helpful in keeping soda machines and product placement ads out of schools. None of this will make you more popular with your children, but popularity polls are for politicians, and the truth is, politicians aren't very popular anyway.

(35) Challenge Media Messages That Suggest That Only Slender Women Have Successful Careers

As if girls didn't feel pressure enough to be rail thin just for the sake of looking good and catching the right guy, they are also being led to believe that if their bodies don't measure up, their future careers will be damaged. Judging from the tall, thin actresses and models who portray police detectives, physicians, scientists, attorneys, corporate heads, politicians, professors, journalists, and numerous other professionals, if a woman is to be successful, she must be thin and shapely. That's certainly the message on television's *Ally McBeal, Sex and the City,* and *Friends,* and in films such as *Charlie's Angels.*

These images of the beautiful and svelte, which can also be found on children's Internet sites and cartoon programs, seem to be cropping up all around us, including in major magazines. In the summer of 2000, Roberta Smith, a *New York Times* critic, observed that a spate of photographs and feature stories of "white, thin, and pretty" women artists had been cropping up in *Vanity Fair, Harper's Bazaar,* and other publications, while a noted artist with a "less sylphlike form" was getting far less attention. Smith pointed out that the slender twenty- and thirty-something artists were often captured in carefully orchestrated images that suggested that for women, at least, "it may take more than the usual amounts of glamour, sex appeal and physical attractiveness to be a successful artist these days. And the more exposed the flesh the better."[7]

The best way to help your daughter understand that contrary to media messages, successful women come in a range of body sizes and shapes, is to treat her to a dose of healthy reality. For this we borrow an idea from the highly successful Take Our Daughters to Work Day, in which millions of girls miss a day at school each year so they can accompany their parents to work. Over the course of a school year, you can take your daughter to meet different women in various positions that may interest her. These excursions will allow her to see a realistic range of women of various ages and body sizes who are highly successful in their chosen careers.

You can use your networking skills to compile a list of women friends and acquaintances who work in various fields. Visits can take place during outings that include you and your daughter, or you can invite some of her friends or members of a girls' group to which she may belong. The advantage of inviting others, of course, is that this translates into more contacts.

Once the woman you've contacted agrees to let your daughter visit her at work, try to select nonholiday dates, such as teacher workdays, when your daughter is not expected in class but when most offices and businesses are in regular operation.

On the way home from the outing, you can challenge the media's image of successful women by asking your daughter what there was about this woman that she found surprising. It's not unusual for children to respond with comments such as, "I was surprised that she was so small" or "I didn't think a Chinese woman would ever do that." Of course, other girls may see past physical aspects and home in on something else entirely. One girl who went to see a woman judge presiding over a federal bankruptcy court said the experience had been akin "to watching grown-ups play a game of 'giant step.' The men [the lawyers who happened to be presenting cases] weren't allowed to approach the bench without the judge's permission. It was way cool."

(36) Teach Her That Our Notion of the "Perfect Body" Is Ephemeral

You can help your daughter take more pleasure in her body, rather than struggle to strive for the popular culture's ideal, by explaining that body standards can precipitously change. You may start by showing her a picture (perhaps from an encyclopedia or on the Internet) of the popular World War II–era illustrations of Rosie the Riveter, generally depicted with powerful biceps. Then show her a picture of Marilyn Monroe, from the postwar era, who had a softer, more sexy image. Conclude with one of the thinner movie stars who later became popular, such as Natalie Wood.

Share your own experiences of trying to keep up with changing body preferences. One fifteen-year-old girl was taken aback at how standards change, when her mother explained that during her youth she'd refused to run track despite being a good runner, because she worried about getting unsightly muscles in her legs.

Some of us came of age when the small-breasted, slim-hipped Twiggy was considered an ideal. Others first fretted over our bodies when models like Cheryl Tiegs represented the 1970s ideal of full breasts and narrow hips. And most mothers remember that in the 1980s it was no longer sufficient simply to be slim. Women who sought "perfect" bodies had to be lean and taut, with muscles toned like Madonna's.

Before the close of the century, the stakes had been raised again. Women were told the perfect body had "muscles of steel." A far cry from the zaftig figures of the 1940s, today's ideal is not only lean and strong, but may include backs ridged with muscles and thighs that professional runners would envy. Looking to the future, a modeling consultant recently proclaimed that the "next new thing in women's bodies" would be "curves, rounder hips and buns, and tiny waists." Ask your daughter to consider how the phrase "next new thing in women's bodies" sounds like an advertising pitch for automobiles or other products.

(37) Explain the Transformation Celebrities and Models Undergo to Become "Camera Ready"

To discourage your daughter from measuring her body against illusions created by the media, you can help her understand that images of celebrities represent only an illusion of beauty. In one of Elane's women's psychology courses, a young woman who had modeled as a teenager talked about the enormous effort required to look "camera ready," a concept our daughters ought to know about.

Movie stars and models are often attractive individuals (most of whom are thin, since many people in the beauty industry believe that slender people look best in photographs). These individuals are used like canvases upon which makeup artists, hair stylists, and fashion designers can create an illusion. If we were observing a young woman being prepared for a photograph, most of us would be surprised at the effort required.

A stylist and an assistant blow-dries, trims, and styles her tresses; sometimes extra hair is woven in for fullness or she is asked to wear a wig. Next, her face is redesigned with cosmetics. Blemishes, freckles, and shadows are concealed, and a base coat is applied. Her eyebrows are shaped and darkened. The color of her eyes may be temporarily changed with contact lenses. Her eyes are then accentuated with liners and shadows, her cheekbones highlighted, her lips outlined and painted. Sometimes lashes are glued onto her eyelashes and then curled and lengthened with mascara. A final dusting of powder minimizes shine.

The young woman then steps into clothes that a wardrobe assistant may pin or sew from the back, to show the body at its most flattering. Lights are adjusted to enhance the look. During photo sessions that can last for hours, hundreds of shots are taken. One is selected and may be altered with the use of a computer program that allows skin, eyes, eyebrows, or other features from different models to be "patched" onto the photo. This supposedly natural shot is used in a magazine or on a billboard or CD cover. Movie stars undergo similar transformations, but sometimes they also use body doubles.

Explain to your daughter that some people confuse these photographic illusions with reality. Draw a parallel with children of the 1950s who became so caught up with the television images of Superman that they tied towels around their shoulders and hurled themselves down flights of stairs believing they could fly.

(38) Limit Fashion Magazines in Your Home

OK, call us humorless, but we want you to know that we see fashion magazines as potentially dangerous to your daughter's health. Like so much of today's media, they're filled with images that underscore the message that women's bodies exist for the entertainment and profit of others. We are intentionally distinguishing between these and other publications. While we are not promoting magazines that focus on celebrity features, we do believe that one benefit of those publications is that they offer insights into what makes a particular individual tick, such as biographical details and interests. These celebrity stories can give readers ideas about honing special talents or stress the importance of persevering despite obstacles.

Fashion magazines, however, often present young women as beautiful clothing racks. Although these publications are filled with a number of individual models, the range of what's deemed "beautiful" is so narrow that they might well be one face, one body, replicated page after page—giving credence to the false belief that this is what "normal" girls and women look like. It is not uncommon for girls to study the thin bodies in these fashion magazines and then cut out and tape a favorite image into a corner of their mirror or onto the cover of a notebook. With each glance, a girl is reminded of what she is not.

Why do these magazines tug at our daughters' hearts? Well, just consider what happens to you when you flip through the pages of a household-products catalog, even when you have no intention of buying anything. All of a sudden, you see an item you simply must have. Or how about when you're in a supermarket. You know one of those I'm-getting-such-a-little-bit-I-don't-need-a-cart trips. By the time you reach the counter, your arms are loaded with items that you somehow now "need." Scenarios like these occur millions of times a day—it's what keeps the economy going. It's not that we're gullible. Marketing experts devise increasingly sophisticated strategies to seduce consumers, convincing us that we need and must have the objects they're selling.

Our daughters are no different from us as consumers, except that they're even more impressionable. They are deeply affected as they turn page after page of colorful layouts filled with glamorous, reed-thin girls and women. So many girls become convinced that they must have these bodies that thousands are literally dying to achieve the "look." In the spring of 2000, in fact, the British Medical Association issued a report suggesting that the media's obsession with skinniness is largely to blame for an escalating number of eating disorders. The medical organization urged magazine editors to limit "superwaif" images.[8] Your daughter can't afford to wait for voluntary compliance. She needs your intervention now.

If your daughter is the one who buys these magazines, raise her consciousness about superwaifs. Borrowing from the anti-tobacco campaign that urges young people to rip pictures of smokers out of magazines, suggest that she do the same to layouts featuring extremely thin models. You may also point out to her any magazines you come across with feature stories that hypocritically highlight the dangers of eating disorders and then a page or two later include a layout featuring superthin models.

Also encourage her to question and challenge unrealistic stereotypes. Tell her you take umbrage with the fact that—whether in films or magazines or on television—most female stars are uniformly young and thin, while their male counterparts are presented in different ages, sizes, and shapes. This will help your daughter internalize the act of questioning and challenging these stereotypes. Urge her to get involved in the Eating Disorders Awareness and Prevention Media Watchdog program. She can log on to their website (www.edap.org) or phone the organization at (206) 382-3587.

If you or your girl are both unwilling to curb your reading of fashion magazines, create a balance between fantasy and reality. Magazines such *Sports Illustrated for Women* and *Sports Illustrated for Kids* portray girls and women with a wide range of realistic body types and of different ages and races who are actively engaged in life.

It can also help if you try to reframe some of the thin model images so they work to your daughter's advantage. For instance, you can point out features on the models that are similar to your daughter's. For instance, you may say, "She's trying to sell that curling iron for women who want curly hair just like yours." Or pointing at another model, you may say, "Her legs are long like yours. I wonder if she is as good a runner as you are." Or, "Her skin is the same chocolate brown as yours; it makes me want to eat you up." Consider other characteristics, such as posture, freckles, fingernails, or foot arches. Point out attributes that are often missed, whether in models or in your daughter.

Be prepared for teenagers to roll their eyes when you initiate these conversations. One seventeen-year-old whose mother had engaged her in these conversations had a few friends visiting. When her mom entered the room, the girl dramatically grabbed the magazine they'd been reading and sat on it, saying, "I have to hide this, or my mother will be telling me how much my shoulders are like Cindy Crawford's." The only problem was that the other girls began to assure her that her mom was right, and they pointed out several other features, including Crawford's eyebrows, that were similar to the girl's. After her friends left, the mother happened upon her daughter reading another magazine. Neither the mother nor the daughter said a word, but when the girl looked up, she smiled, as if to say, "Thanks, Mom."

(39) Limit Television and Monitor Internet Use

Whenever we make this suggestion, parents throw up their hands in despair. For those of us who are away during the day, limiting what our children tune in to or log on to seems like an impossible chore. But with children ages two to seventeen—who have computers, video games, and television—spending an average of four hours and forty-eight minutes a day in front of some type of screen,[9] it's vital that we take a stand. Keep in mind that television and the Internet offer passive, hypnotic experiences that can keep your daughter from pursuing the kind of active lifestyle necessary for her to maintain a healthy body. Studies indicate that the more a child watches television, the more likely she or he is to be obese and physically unfit.[10]

There's also the content factor to consider. If your child is watching television, for instance, she may be turning into inappropriate fare. The Federal Trade Commission has accused the entertainment industry of deliberately targeting advertising of violent and/or sexually explicit movies, video games, and music to children as young as age ten. And your daughter can be exposed to a lot more than just advertising. Her dialing choices range from music videos, in which semiclothed young women present themselves suggestively, to soap operas, in which girls are often portrayed as making self-defeating choices. And television can cast a powerful spell. With its skilled use of lighting, camera angles, and sound, it can manipulate and influence young viewers. The on-screen characters can seem so realistic that they can affect the way your girl views every aspect of her body—whether measuring herself against others or gauging the way she allows herself to be treated.

In addition the dangers posed to young people using the Internet cannot be understated. Giving your daughter unlimited access would be akin to taking her to a city with which she is unfamiliar and telling her to find her way back home. Of course, you have reason to hope she'll arrive home safely, but you'd also have to accept the fact that she may run into some very harmful people.

Neither medium deserves an "all-or-nothing" approach. It's not necessary to banish television sets. There are some good programs available. One show that comes to mind is the HBO series *The Royal Diaries,* the stories of teenage girls who eventually became powerful rulers, including Cleopatra and Elizabeth I. There are also shows that offer lighter fare and are not only amusing but can serve as conversation starters with peers. And the Internet is not only a great research tool, but it can encourage self-expression (whether a girl is E-mailing friends or "chatting" on message boards).

So discuss with your daughter how much and what kind of

television and computer time is acceptable to you. In Brenda's home, for example, there is no cable service, and the children are allowed three hours of television time per week, which includes video rentals and occasional weekend bonus excerpts from major sports events such as the U.S. Open or the Olympics. The following are more ideas for limiting television and computer use:

- Don't furnish her room with a television or computer.

- Encourage her to look over the television listings and choose shows she wants to watch that fit within your time constraints and guidelines.

- Watch television with younger children and challenge objectionable messages.

- Consider getting a television with a built-in V chip to help enforce your policies.

- Check ratings on computer games and respect them.

- Raise her consciousness about computer games by pointing out violent content or demeaning images of girls and women.

- Learn how to play some of her video games, so you'll understand how she's spending her time.

- Find an Internet provider with features that automatically shut down after a certain time, as well as one that denies access to mature newsgroups or websites.

- Set up her computer in a fairly public family space so you can occasionally look over her shoulder.

- From time to time, check her computer's history files, since these automatically record addresses that have been visited.

(40) Teach Her to Pay Attention to the Song She's Singing

When it comes to criticizing your child's music, allow yourself to be guided by three words: handle with care. For adolescents in particular, music is more than just a mood enhancer. It has the ability to give meaning and intensity to the inexplicable emotions of their lives. Ask teenagers what matters most to them, and after family and God, many will list music. With that in mind, you'll want to avoid any sweeping generalizations ("It all just sounds like a bunch of noise" or "They aren't socially relevant, like the ones I used to listen to").

We're recommending that you tread lightly not solely out of respect for your daughter's emotional needs, but for her physical health as well. Music can be good for her body. It can serve as a catalyst, moving her to laugh, sing, or dance.

At the same time, it's important that you keep an ear open to what she's listening to. The advisories on audiotape and CD packages can be important signals for parents who are concerned with "explicit content." But sometimes these labels don't go far enough. That's why it's up to you to teach your daughter to pay attention to what she's singing.

After all, researchers have found that one way to get people to transform damaging behaviors and thought patterns is to give them positive messages, called affirmations, that they say or write repeatedly with feeling. Researchers have also found that when affirmations are sung, they can be even more effective. Music is that powerful. So it's logical to assume that if we want to create self-abnegating thoughts, we may ask someone to program their subconscious by singing "disaffirmations," that is, denigrating phrases that normalize violent and demeaning behaviors. Your daughter needs to know that she may already be singing disaffirmations in the form of popular lyrics, which can influence her attitudes about how girls should be treated.

For instance, she may be a fan of the rap and hip-hop artist Eminem, who often refers to women as "whores" and whose songs tell of his eagerness to rape and murder them. If so, she may have been mouthing the lyrics to "Kill You," a song that includes the words "guns, knives, wives, nuns, sluts." Then there is the song that has been sung and performed by girls as young as three and four, in which Britney Spears asks to be "hit" once again. After hearing those lyrics, others, including one in which Christine Aguilera asserts that suitors have to know how to "rub" her in the right way or the band Wheatus's description of teenage "dirtbags," sound almost tame.

We realize that songs like these will continue to be produced and sung by young people despite any parental objections. Still, our daughters can only benefit from consciousness-raising. Rather than banning lyrics you find objectionable, point out how demeaning messages in popular songs can negatively alter your daughter's self-image. Even if she doesn't appear to be listening, she will hear you. And when you take into account just how loudly some young people play their music, the fact that she hears you at all is an important start.

(41) Help Her to See Through the Seductive Images of Cigarette Smoking

"My daughter wouldn't smoke," insist many parents. And for those with younger girls, smoking does seem like someone else's problem. But the pressure to smoke increases in middle school. A study conducted by the American Legacy Foundation found that 12.8 percent of newly arriving middle school students said they had never tried tobacco; six months later, that figure had risen to 15.2 percent. According to the Centers for Disease Control, only 8 percent of middle school girls smoke regularly. But by the time our girls reach high school, 28 percent smoke. In fact, each day in the United States about 1,500 girls (and an equal number of boys) develop the habit.

Research indicates that many youngsters start smoking because they have been seduced by images of smokers in films, music videos, and advertising. Despite a major national anti-smoking campaign, too many children still believe it's cool to smoke. A lot of girls also use it as a method of staving off hunger because they hope to remain thin. Most don't expect to become addicted to nicotine, and since young people often see themselves as invincible, they almost certainly don't expect to die from tobacco-related diseases.

Most youngsters believe they can quit smoking whenever they want, but research indicates that girls who begin smoking as teenagers continue for an average of twenty years,[11] more than enough time to damage their bodies. There are even more far-reaching implications for tobacco-related risks. According to the Centers for Disease Control, teenagers who smoke cigarettes are three times more likely than nonsmokers to use marijuana and twenty-two times more likely to use cocaine. They are also more likely to engage in unprotected sex.

In the face of all this unsettling information, it helps to know that there is much that we can do as parents to help our children choose to not smoke. As you continue reading this book, you will find that many of the suggestions that stress fitness will aid in keeping your daughter tobacco-free. The following are other specific tips:

- **Refuse to buy candy cigarettes:** According to a report in the *British Medical Journal,* for more than six decades the tobacco industry has given its tacit support to companies that make candy cigarettes to encourage children to smoke. The article also alleged that one U.S. candy maker concealed its own research that suggested that children who eat candy cigarettes were more likely to become smokers, by allowing children to practice smoking behaviors.[12]

- **Read about it:** Pick up a copy of *How to Help Your Kids Choose to Be Tobacco Free: A Guide for Parents of Children Ages 3 Through 19,* by Dr. Robert Schwebel. It's the best book available on the subject.

- **Share your story:** If you smoke, you're probably already aware that your daughter is likely to follow in your footsteps.

Do work at quitting, and tell your daughter how difficult it is to quit once you get hooked.

- **Spell out short-term consequences:** Tell your girl that smoking will affect her athletic ability. And if she's interested in boys, show her a personal ads section in the paper, in which men who describe the kind of women they desire often include the words "no smokers." Tell her that boys usually feel the same way. Explain that smoking causes bad breath and can yellow teeth.

- **Watch her friends:** If her friends smoke, she's more likely to become a smoker too.

- **Allow room for candor:** Promise your daughter that if she does start smoking, if she admits it you will not punish her for telling you.

- **Alert her to the media message:** Challenge her to keep count of the number of times in one week that she spots a media image that promotes smoking. And encourage her to rip smoking ads (or any pictures that glorify smoking) out of her magazines.

- **Mobilize school support:** Work with your parent-teacher association to start a no-smoking program at your daughter's school. For help, contact your local branch of the American Cancer Society.

VI

Acceptance and Reconciliation

Puberty as the Adolescent "Change of Life"

Although it is no longer unusual to hear women talking about their "change of life," we seldom hear this term applied to pubescent girls. Yet this is a time in your daughter's life when she will experience such sweeping changes that she may feel she has awakened in someone else's body. Our goal in this work is not just for you to help your daughter feel comfortable with her "new" self, but actually to be grateful for it.

(42) Learn About Early Puberty

As the mother of twin girls, Lorraine had immersed herself in parenting books, determined to prepare herself for all her daughters' developmental stages. But she eventually realized that nothing she had come across helped her to cope with the physical changes that her daughters experienced at eight years old: the girls developed breasts and pubic hair. Two years later they began to menstruate.

"I cried," Lorraine said. "I felt I'd done something wrong." The experiences of Lorraine's daughters are more common than one might expect. On the average, girls in the United States begin to menstruate at age twelve, but some begin as early as eight and nine years old. One report suggests that early puberty is experienced by an estimated one in seven Caucasian girls, and that there may be an even higher incidence among African American girls.[1] This phenomenon has been linked to everything from obesity to hormones in cow's milk, beef, and chicken, to environmental chemicals, to electric lights, and to the absence of a father in the home. There is no definitive answer as to why it is occurring.

If your daughter is showing signs of early puberty, it's important that you not get caught up in these unfounded ideas. If you panic about her body, so will she. Yes, early puberty can be inconvenient and somewhat alarming. But consider the larger picture. Perhaps you already know that when the female body is exposed to high stress and starvation, reproductive functioning can shut down. It's the body's way of ensuring that a child isn't conceived during less than optimal times. Conversely, early puberty may be nature's response to improved conditions, including better nutrition. A body undergoing early puberty, then, is somewhat like a hothouse flower, which in response to lighting and soil nutrients blooms out of season. But while a girl may be maturing on the outside, she can still be a child on the inside. Fortunately, there is much you can do to help her continue to feel good about her body. The following are some suggestions:

- **Normalize changes:** Explain that many other girls are experiencing similar changes. With this in mind, don't nix sleepovers because you want to hide the truth from others. Your daughter will feel your shame about her body and internalize it.

- **Consult her pediatrician:** Sometimes early puberty is caused by medical problems. There is also a possibility that it may affect your daughter's ultimate height. Her pediatrician may recommend hormone treatments that can temporarily halt sexual development. As with any long-term treatment, you will want to consider carefully whether this is the right course for your daughter.

- **Explain the birds and the bees:** Signs of puberty mean it's time for you to discuss the facts of life with her. This means that unlike many parents, you won't be waiting too late to initiate important conversations about sex. Keep the details simple.

- **Call your health care provider:** These companies are sometimes cooperative when it comes to setting up information sessions and workshops for parents and children.

(43) Prepare Her Mentally for Her "New" Body

In addition to the menstrual cycle, puberty changes include the development of breasts, growth of underarm and pubic hair, and the expansion of fat cells. In fact, a girl may gain as much as forty pounds in a year. One girl described the experience as "morphing" into a stranger's body. You (or an older sister, grandmother, or godmother) can prepare your girl for puberty changes by working with her on an art project created especially for prepubescent girls:

Supplies
- a photograph depicting you at about the same age as your girl, placed in an envelope

- crayons, markers, or colored pencils

- three sheets of heavy, unlined paper, 8 × 11 inches

- yarn (the color of your hair)

- liquid glue or a glue gun

- feathers, sparkles, or other decorative items

Ask your daughter to help you create a picture of you when you're feeling happy. It can be fun to add touches that capture your personal interests, such as a tennis racket, musical notes, flowers, and so forth. Glue on yarn for hair and sparkles for earrings. Don't worry about artistic excellence. A stick figure is fine, if that's all she can draw. As the two of you work together, explain why you love the body you now have. When you have finished, write at the top of the paper, "After Puberty" and explain that you haven't always looked this way. Take the photograph from the envelope and show her what you used to look like.

Tell her what you liked about being a girl. Next you can explain that puberty starts when the hypothalamus in the brain sends a signal to the pituitary gland. That's when the ovaries begin to make estrogen, a hormone that eventually causes the body to become more womanly. Perhaps you can share a few of your memories about puberty, when you may have grown taller or developed rounder hips and fuller breasts.

Now the two of you can work on a drawing that depicts who your girl is now. As you work together, ask her to tell you what she likes about being a girl. After adding flourishes to the page that help define who she is, write her name at the top of the page, add the date, and write in bold letters, "Before Puberty."

When you have finished, tell her that although you can draw a picture of what she looks like now, the two of you can only guess what she'll look like after puberty. Tell her that you do know that she'll be awesome because she's such a wonderful girl now. Ask her to tell you some of the fun activities she may enjoy when she's older and has more of a "big girl's" body. When you have finished, you my want to give her a hug and tell her that although people change, it's nice to know that she will always be your girl and that you'll always be connected.

Although some girls ages eleven and older may enjoy this art project, others may be more interested in learning about puberty through books, such as the classic and informative *What's Happening to My Body? Book for Girls,* by Linda Madaras. High-school-age girls will enjoy the ultracool *Deal With It! A Whole New Approach to Your Body, Brain and Life as a Gurl,* by Esther Drill, Heather McDonald, and Rebecca Odes. This book is filled with frank and saucy information, as well as excerpts of conversations from the popular website www.GURL.com. If you're looking for a book for a teenager's independent reading, consider *It's My Life!: A Power Journal for Teens,* by Tian Dayton, Ph.D. This workbook provides wonderful opportunities for your girl to come to terms with the many changes that are occurring in her life.

(44) Calm Her Fears About Her Physical Inheritance

Probably as long as your daughter can remember, she has been hearing how much she resembles one or both of her parents. That notion can be comforting, but when a pubescent girl's features begin changing, she may take a look at the people in her family and start to feel as if there's a big roulette wheel spinning that will determine the way she'll look. She may start worrying that she'll inherit the "heavy" legs that her mom and aunts may have or the "double" chin that runs in dad's family or the "terrible" acne that her older sister struggled with.

Girls may also start to worry about being "just like" someone in the family who is obese. And there is certainly a rationale for these concerns. Research indicates that if one parent is obese, there is a 40 percent chance the child will be too; if both parents are obese, there is an 80 percent likelihood that the child will be obese also. These results may be partially explained by the connection between weight and family lifestyles, but studies of twins raised separately have consistently indicated that genetics plays an important role in determining obesity.

None of this means, of course, that your daughter is going to look like a clone of you or any other family member. She will have her own unique body. There are certain strategies that you can use to ease your daughter's fears about how she will ultimately look, such as these:

- **Don't reinforce her fears:** If you say, for example, that she's bound to be "big" because "everyone" in the family is "big," she will feel as if the Sword of Damocles is hanging over her head. Words, such as "you'll always be big," are so powerful that a girl can internalize them and unconsciously work hard to ensure that they come true. Instead, tell your daughter that while people do inherit family body types, she can choose to be a healthy example of that body type.

- **Help her feel connected to the positive nuances of her ancestry:** Choose positive aspects of your ancestry that can help her feel more comfortable with her changing body. Consider, for example, how a girl who is several inches taller than her classmates may feel her height is an advantage after she sees photos of her tall Swedish relatives. Another girl, who feels clumsy and awkward as she adjusts to her changing body, may enjoy hearing that her French ancestors were known for their elegance and fashion flair.

- **Construct a family body tree:** Rather than a careful delineation of who begat whom, a family body tree is an art project she can hang on her wall. It will allow her to laugh at her discomfort about inherited features. You will need the following:

Supplies
1. Art paper or brown wrapping paper that is as wide and as long as your daughter's body from head to toe, with her arms extended.

2. Xeroxed copies of relatives' photos, particularly full body shots.

3. Scissors, glue, crayons, a pencil, a black marking pen, and the lid from a round plastic food container.

Instructions
1. Spread paper on the floor, and with your daughter on her back, with her arms five inches away from her hips and her feet five inches apart, trace her body outline. When you have finished, cut out the figure so you have what could be described as a paper shape of her shadow.

2. Draw and color in her features.

3. Trace some circles on paper and cut them out. The number of circles you cut will depend on how many family members' photos you have assembled.

4. Choose a picture of a relative and trim away everything but this person's face and body; then glue it to a paper circle, leaving space to write.

5. In the circle, write a silly description of one characteristic of each relative. For example, one man told his daughter about her grandmother's excellent hearing (super ears) that made it impossible for him to sneak out at night and join his friends for drag races; a mother

told about her sister's "steel toenails" that scratched her legs when they shared a bed.

As you will explain to your daughter, saying someone has long blond hair, for instance, doesn't really tell you anything about whether this is a good or a bad person, interesting or dull, honest or dishonest, or any of the important things that make us unique. Tell her that making assumptions about a person based on their appearance is a trap that many people fall into.

6. After completing your circles, glue them to respective areas of your daughter's paper form.

The laughter that this activity will elicit will go a long way toward neutralizing any concerns your daughter may have about her genetic heritage.

(45) Acknowledge Any Grief She May Feel About the Loss of Her Girlish Body

When girls enter puberty, many parents are unprepared for the grief that can accompany this dramatic change of life. As a result, some girls aren't given an opportunity to work through their feelings, and they remain locked in a semipermanent case of the blues. Make no mistake about it, grief is more than one emotion; it includes anger, sadness, guilt, and fear, as well as feelings of confusion and disorientation. Some girls act out their grief, turning against their own bodies by using drugs, alcohol, and tobacco. And grief can also affect a girl's relationship with food, as she tries to unconsciously soothe, numb, or punish herself by over- or undereating. Some grief-filled girls may engage in cutting (attacking their bodies with razors or glass shards), inappropriate and early sex, or thoughts of suicide. Grief can be seen in a girl's body. You may notice slumped shoulders, dull eyes, or lethargic movements. Your pubescent daughter may be especially irritable—which may be connected to hormonal changes.

Some of this grief is connected to society's obsession with thinness, causing our daughters to deeply feel the loss of their little-girl bodies. Many have been narrow hipped, with slender arms and thighs—bodies that are close to the ideal that's touted in the media. But pubescent girls often develop rounder hips and fuller, womanly figures. It may seem to some that they have suddenly become targets for ridicule or inappropriate attention from boys and men. Even if everyone in the family is extremely sensitive, pubescent girls often compare themselves to thin images in the media and feel unworthy. In fact, many psychologists view anorexia as an unconscious attempt to regain the girlish form.

In addition to this issue, Tian Dayton, Ph.D., a psychologist specializing in issues related to grief, trauma, and addiction, believes that adolescents grieve the loss of childhood pleasures and the approach of adult responsibilities. For girls raised by mothers who are the family workhorses, a woman's responsibilities may seem even less appealing.

Grief must run its course, but girls who are going through this difficult time can be helped with many of the interventions we've included in this book, including finding healthy expressions for anger and sorrow. Again, parental closeness is of tremendous importance. The problem, said Dayton, is that children often push their parents away during this period, even though they want to remain close. "Kids need to know the parent is hovering in the background with their best interests in mind, she said. "The parent is the lighthouse. That's how a child navigates her way through the grief of adolescence. If you step back too far, your child can be lost to you."

Fathers can help by setting an appropriate tone that allows for a continuation of support. As a girl's body becomes more full figured, fathers often handle their discomfort by emotionally disappearing from their daughters' lives. Striking the right balance is a delicate dance for fathers, but one that can be learned only through trial and error.

Mothers, of course, should work hard to maintain a connection as well. Weekend mother-daughter trips can allow time for bonding, rest, and reflection. During these times, you can encourage your girl to do most of the talking, with a method called "reflective listening." Suppose your daughter says, for instance, "My life sucks." Rather than rush to try to cheer her up, you might say, "I've certainly felt that way from time to time. What part of your life bothers you?" Keep the tone light but not superficial.

Sometimes when pubescent girls are irritable, getting a conversation going with them may not seem all that attractive. Showing affection may be even more difficult. Nevertheless, we urge you to find times when you can be physically demonstrative toward her. Your girl needs your loving touch to thrive. It helps to remember that demonstrations of love don't always have to be spontaneous (although those are nice, too). One mother, who said she felt a physical aversion to her fourteen-year-old daughter, "who, in a matter of months became this angry, defiant little monster," began to plan times when she could connect with her girl. "I noticed that when our family goes to church together, she leans into me, and then I feel affectionate toward her. So now I look forward to those times when we can snuggle." Other parents have found that massaging an adolescent's shoulder muscles offers another opportunity for a loving touch. If you give her a shoulder rub, ask her to massage yours as well.

Finally, as you continue to support her in grieving the loss of her girlhood, don't give in to unsympathetic others who insist you're indulging her. Kids don't suddenly turn into "brats." Your daughter can't simply put grief behind her and move on. You'll know when it is no longer in her body: it will show in the spring of her step, the light will return to her eyes, and she'll stand tall in her womanly self.

(46) Send Her to School with a Blush Bag

At a time when your girl is feeling highly sensitive about her body, any unusual occurrence can be a major cause of embarrassment. With just a little advance planning, you can fill a small makeup bag with items that she can use in a pinch so she can feel comfortable about her body when she's away from home.

Though it may be tempting to use a plastic sandwich bag to hold items, we advise against it. Since you can see through these bags, your daughter will just get caught up in worrying about whether some boy will spot an item and tease her. Makeup bags can be found at a range of prices. Talk with your daughter about what to include. Here are a few suggestions:

- a covered sanitary napkin

- a small comb

- a small tube of hair gel

- a blemish concealer

- two safety pins

- a needle and a flat packet of thread

- a Q-tip

- spot remover

- over-the-counter antiflatulence tablets

- a roll of breath mints

- a small bottle of deodorant

- asthma medication (or any prescription medication that she requires)

- emergency money, including some quarters (for a cab, telephone call, and the like)

Your daughter can restock this bag twice a semester, adding and taking out items that meet her needs.

(47) Take a Mother-Daughter Shopping Trip

Many girls and women love to shop. It's a great narcissistic activity, and a few hours of shopping together, with plans for a cup of tea or snack, can be a ritual that helps welcome womanhood. This is not the same thing as handing over money and sending your daughter on her own. By accompanying her, you not only have a chance to share giggles and the excitement of finding a bargain, but she may feel encouraged to discuss with you any anxieties she may have about her body.

Also, depending on how well you're getting along at the time, your daughter might appreciate hearing constructive feedback from you about the clothes she's trying on. And yes, contrary to what you may have heard, it's OK to tell your daughter that she's beautiful. Some people believe this can lead a girl to be overly focused on her looks. But telling your girl that she's "lovely" or "gorgeous" or "a knockout" is another way of saying you love her. Still, if you're uncomfortable with dwelling on your daughter's physical attributes, mention her inner strengths as well. As she tries on a pair of jeans or zips up what may become her prom dress, you might say, for instance, "Wow, you're gorgeous as well as brilliant!" Besides, anyone who looks at her body under the unflattering light of most fitting rooms can use a dose of Mommy love and reassurance. Your daughter may also enjoy posing for you in clothes she selects.

If the day also includes some anger, try to take it in stride. This is real life, not the movies, and the truth is, even times such as these may not be as affection filled as you'd like. What's important is that you're signaling that you want to be there for her and that you treasure her even when she is having a hard time feeling good about herself.

VII

Body Image
How She Sees Herself

There's a greeting card that depicts a scrawny chicken staring into a looking glass, and what's reflected back is a resplendent peacock. The words read "It's what you see that counts." When it comes to our daughters' bodies, that message couldn't be more on target. Perhaps you can recall looking through old snapshots and realizing that you really did look pretty good, just as someone who loved you had insisted. Sometimes you may even think about how different your life might have been if only you'd been able to see that yourself. Now it's your turn to give your daughter opportunities to see herself with love.

(48) Give Her a Full-Length Mirror and Flattering Lights

For your darling daughter, you'll need a mirror, but not just any old one hung in any old place. A high-quality full-length mirror that does not distort will allow your daughter to get a good sense of what she looks like in the buff or fully clothed. It should be hung or mounted in a room where she can lock the door and enjoy long stretches of privacy, a bedroom or bathroom perhaps. When puberty begins, she will be hesitant to disrobe if she can't be ensured privacy. If she has only a small mirror over the bathroom sink, she has to guess what the rest of her body looks like. And guessing, particularly when her body is undergoing dramatic changes, can be disturbing.

Wherever you decide to hang her mirror, you should give careful consideration to how the room is illuminated. Fortunately, there are now many lighting stores where you can get professional advice. Steve Strauss, a lighting designer from Light Forms in Manhattan, says that fluorescent bulbs are the most harsh and unflattering, while newer, more complimentary lighting tends to be color balanced and closer to natural sunlight.

Why go to all this trouble? When people look at themselves in mirrors under flattering lights, they have a better chance of seeing themselves the way people who love them do, explained John Conger, Ph.D., a bioenergetic therapist in Berkeley, California. "A girl might look at herself in the mirror and notice the big mole on her chin, or think she should have a child's body without breasts, instead of her new fuller figure. But when loved ones see her, what they notice most of all is her emotional energy. Good lighting can correct negative self-images. And just as someone who has broad hips might look better in a solid-colored, A-line skirt, rather than a plaid, boxy one, lights can flatter."

A full-length mirror with the right lighting can be magical, reflecting your daughter when she is at her most confident as well as her most vulnerable. Putting up a mirror when she is between eighteen months and two years is not too soon. This is a period when she still considers herself an extension of you and will enjoy seeing herself as powerful. As she matures and realizes she is a separate, smaller being—a development stage Conger refers to as "the birth of appearance"—she may feel a little timid but still glance into the mirror, notice her body, and joyfully execute a pirouette.

By her eighth birthday, she may stand before the mirror, boyish in frame, bold in spirit, shyer in her nakedness but still more interested in the world than her body. Five years later, at thirteen, she may stare fixedly into the reflecting glass, but only after making certain that the lock on the door is turned. She wants no judgmental eyes but her own on this body. Completely exposed, she will take measure of herself as an almost woman. And if you have helped her to love this body, the magical, silent sentry is there still, reflecting back a young woman who, in naked joy, may execute another pirouette.

(49) Let Her Use the Family Video Camera to Document Her Life

Pull out, rent, or borrow a video camera and present it to your daughter, along with an extra videotape. Include a note or card explaining that you would like her to tape the story of her life. She can shoot the video at her school and in her neighborhood, and her friends can handle the camera and get shots of her.

If she agrees, the fruits of her labor can be shared at a family gathering, during a sleepover, or when visiting grandparents. When you watch it with her, you'll find that this is a gift for both of you. For you, it offers a window into her world: how she sounds, moves, and looks in relation to others. And she will be able to see, from one more perspective, who she is becoming.

(50) Ask Her to Teach You Something Physical That You Can't Do

From tying shoes to catching a ball to riding a bike—mothers and fathers are usually the teachers in the parent-child relationship. However, your daughter will jump at the chance to reverse roles. Let her teach you a skill she has mastered and it will help her see herself as physically adept.

When Karen, the mother of seventeen-year-old Samantha, asked her daughter to teach her something physical, Samantha volunteered to teach her how to throw a punch. "One reason Sam enjoyed it so much," Karen speculated, "is because she got to laugh at me and call me names. She said I was a 'wuss,' and that I couldn't fight my way out of a plastic bag. She loved it. I never did learn to do it right, but it did make me realize, though, how hard it must be to always be sitting in the learner's seat."

There was an added plus to their punching lesson. For the past five years, Karen and Samantha's relationship had been marked by tension. Samantha blamed her mother for her parents' divorce, so their moments of closeness were few and far between. In fact, Karen thinks Samantha chose to demonstrate punching because what she really wanted to do was knock her mother's block off (even though no one was hurt).

When the two engaged in this lesson, they were on the front lawn, with Samantha standing behind her mother and guiding her fist. Karen realized it had been months since the two had even touched. "And we had never done anything physical and fun together. That had been her father's domain." Karen said that coming in close contact with her daughter brought tears to her eyes, and she began to empathize with Samantha. "I hadn't allowed myself to feel how sad she must be. Mike may have been a lousy husband, but he was a good father, and now he lives across the country from us. She must have felt miserable."

What can your daughter teach you? She is sure to surprise you. Even young children can teach you a favorite somersault or how to jump rope or touch your nose with your foot or roar like a favorite animal. The sudden turn of the tables will remind you both how good it feels to play together.

(51) If You're Slimmer than She Is, Don't Wear the Clothes She Has Outgrown

In a world in which slimmer is considered better, slender mothers who wear clothes that their adolescent daughters have outgrown are setting up a no-win situation. No matter how slender she may become, there is the risk that she will forever see herself as having a body that's inferior to mom's.

Andrea, a twenty-seven-year-old ballet dancer, recalls that when she was a lead dancer in a local Nutcracker production more than fifteen years ago, her mother showed up at a rehearsal wearing a costume that Andrea could no longer fit into. "Even before I knew she was standing nearby, I heard the buzz from the others. She was quite beautiful and took tremendous pride in being so slender. I was under a lot of stress and had put on a little weight, a fact of which I was painfully aware." Unlike other mothers, who were picking up their children after rehearsal, her mother had walked onto the stage, when she should have waited in the audience. When Andrea spun around and saw her mother, she was horrified. "Mom looked the way I knew I should."

Although Andrea eventually grew taller and more slender, she said her mother always remained thinner, "and this was something she quietly lorded over me with my clothes." After Andrea moved away from home to attend college and her mother visited her at the dorm, "Mom put on one of my blouses and then just walked around with it hanging from her petite body. . . . Very funny, right?" Andrea believes that as a result of incidents such as these, she began to see herself as "fat" and she said that she still struggles with this image. Now she has a daughter of her own. The child is only seven, but Andrea is already making plans for how she'll handle "any clothing problems" during her adolescence. "Anything she outgrows will go straight to Goodwill. I'm determined to spare her the heartache."

In the past, or so it seems, if there was a female in the family struggling with weight, it was generally the pubescent girl's mother. From our observation, that's not necessarily true today. Although many American adults are gaining weight, many of the mothers we know work hard at maintaining slender, healthy bodies. In fact, the percentage of women and men over forty-five who are lifting weights has more than doubled since 1995.[1] At the same time, American children are 20 percent heavier than children raised during the 1950s. *New York Times* health columnist Jane Brody writes, "The fitness bug that bit many adults has not carried over to the younger generation."[2]

Some slimmer mothers have found that they have to tread carefully. Being slimmer than a daughter is a scenario that can be fraught with tension. The daughter may complain that other people are making unflattering comparisons, or she may feel her mother loves her less for being "imperfect." The situation is compounded if one daughter resembles a heavyset parent while a sister has the body shape of a more slender parent.

If you have a similar discrepancy in your home, wait for your daughter to bring it up, and most likely she will. Then let her do most of the talking. Keep in mind that the reason she's initiating the conversation is that she wants to hear you reassure her about how she looks now, not how she may look in the future. Telling her, for instance, "Don't worry, you'll grow out of this" will only make the situation worse. It does help, however, to point out that, *of course,* you have different bodies. After all, you can add, she's your daughter, not your clone. By communicating to her that you're delighted that she's an individual in her own right, she will feel that she has a body that's different but not in competition with yours.

(52) Teach Adopted and Multiracial Girls to Love Features That Are Different from Mommy's

Lisa is a thirty-two-year-old blond, blue-eyed European American who is married to a Japanese American. Their seven-year-old daughter, Anne, looks a lot like her dad. With thick black hair and an olive complexion, she's a beautiful girl, but Lisa worries that her daughter doesn't believe it. "My daughter wants to look like me. She hates her hair. I've been trying to figure out what I've done to make her reject her Asian features."

Lisa is certainly not alone in grappling with this issue. There are now millions of multiracial children in the United States, and thousands of other youngsters are adopted each year by parents who are of a different race.[3] Looking different from one's parents because of ethnic features can be a highly sensitive issue. Children generally view their mothers as the epitome of beauty, and young girls develop an internalized sense of themselves based on their image of their mothers.

The problem is even more complicated in Western society, which venerates a narrow, Nordic standard of beauty. For that reason, children of various races, including those whose mothers look just like them, often long for physical features that neither they nor their mothers have, including blue eyes and blond hair. In families in which girls look racially different from their mothers, this situation is compounded. Despite pressures, however, there are ways to help your multiracial or adopted girl see herself as beautiful. Here are some suggestions:

· **Hair length:** If your girl's hair texture is different from yours and you don't know how to care for it, don't chop it off because it's difficult for you to style. You'll give her the impression that her hair is unacceptable. Instead, find women who have similar locks and ask for advice.

- **Hair texture:** If your daughter's hair is straight, don't use permanents to make it curly; if it's very curly, don't straighten it. These are decisions girls should make when they are mature enough to care for their own hair. Chemical treatments can damage hair. Again, the message conveyed is that her hair as it is isn't acceptable.

- **Responses:** If some thoughtless person says your daughter looks nothing like you, you and your girl will feel a lot better if you have thought of a response in advance. You may say something upbeat, such as, "Really? We're so close that I can certainly see myself in her."

- **Playgroups:** If you're raising her in a neighborhood in which there are few other children who look like her, use networking skills to organize a playgroup with children of the same race or ethnicity.

- **Collage:** Collect magazine pictures of women with features similar to your daughter's and encourage her to construct a collage for her wall.

(53) Remember That White Girls Aren't the Only Ones Whose Self-Images Suffer from the Blitz of Commercial Images

Sixteen-year-old Elizabeth, five feet nine and only eighty-five pounds, saw herself as being horribly overweight. She was clearly anorexic, but she was close to death before her parents realized that she had literally stopped eating. How had her parents missed all the signals? Elizabeth's mom said, "I just didn't think this was something that happens to black girls." Their family physician, a European American, also resisted the notion that Elizabeth was anorexic. He admitted that he had been "blinded" to her symptoms because he had always heard that "most African American women are happy with their bodies."

Like so many people, Elizabeth's mother and her physician had bought into myths. Although it's true that disordered eating certainly affects a disproportionately higher number of affluent European American females, it is hardly restricted to any one racial group, socioeconomic class, or gender. Yet misconceptions and stereotypes about body types of various racial groups continue to be perpetuated.

Some Latina girls, for instance, are unhappy with their bodies because they believe all Latinas should have big breasts. Some Asian girls are unhappy with their frames because they believe all Asian females are supposed to be petite. Some European American girls believe their bottoms are too big because all white girls are supposed to have "flat" bottoms. Racial stereotypes about bodies can cause girls to see their bodies as flawed and can lead them to diet and/or exercise obsessively. And as in Elizabeth's case, these stereotypes may blind health care practitioners to problems.

Despite these misconceptions, you do have to wonder how otherwise reasonable people have been blinded to the truth about African American girls and eating disorders. The misunderstanding can be traced back to the early 1990s when a study found that 90 percent of white females versus 30 percent of African American females reported being dissatisfied with their bodies. The news of African American female body satisfaction was widely disseminated by the media. And since there is a greater tolerance in the African American community for heavier female bodies, the idea of African American female body satisfaction seemed to make sense. But from this point on, things began to snowball as one stereotype was added to another.

Unfortunately, many people in the larger culture view African Americans as a monolithic group. The African American community does tend to have a high incidence of obesity; approximately 66 percent of African American women, compared with 47 percent of white women, are overweight.[4] This has led some people to believe that practically all black women are overweight. Having heard about the high body-satisfaction study, some people have also become convinced that most African American women are comfortable being overweight. Finally, by accepting the anorexia-only-happens-to-rich-white-girls myth, they began to believe that African American females aren't prone to eating disorders.

That hodgepodge of beliefs may help explain why, about five years ago, when Pamela Scott-Johnson, Ph.D., a psychologist at the historically black Spelman College in Atlanta, began researching bulimia and anorexia among African American women, people told her, "This is a nonissue. This doesn't happen to black women." She was hearing a different story from counselors at other historically black colleges who were "seeing girls who were obviously suffering from eating disturbances. People didn't know what to make of it."

Scott-Johnson has since carried out a small-scale study among African Americans in the Atlanta area and found symptoms of undereating among a small percentage of the girls and women she interviewed. Approximately 10 percent of the black undereaters identified in her study were bulimic or anorexic. Scott-Johnson also found a slightly higher incidence of women bingeing and starving themselves, something many of the interviewees described as "fasting" or "colon cleansing." She has been unable to obtain funding for a more in-depth study. She says that many white researchers already have their minds made up that most African Americans are fat. "There is little support for the notion that some of us may be undereating."

How does she explain the high level of satisfied black women in body-image studies? Scott-Johnson believes that current research is Euro-centered and doesn't take into account cultural differences among African Americans. With similar concerns in mind, in 1994, *Essence* magazine commissioned its own eating disorder survey. Clinical researchers concluded from the 2,000 responses that African American women were at risk and suffering from eating disorders in the same proportions as white women.[5]

Another psychologist working on this issue, Shanette Harris, Ph.D., who teaches at the University of Rhode Island, has her own theory about the discrepancy between what's actually occurring in the African American community versus what's reflected in the major body-image studies. Harris suggested that many of the African American women who are interviewed in body-image studies may intentionally try to sound more accepting of their bodies than they actually are. "African American women are scripted to say positive things about themselves in public because there's so much negativity out there about us already." Harris also stressed that it's important to consider that interviewers in these studies are often white and this, too, affects what African American women will reveal. "Black women are not going to sit in front of the very women they've been told are the models of physical perfection and criticize their own lives or their bodies." The social class of the interviewer is another factor to consider. Harris believes that if a black, middle-class woman is interviewing women of the same race who are working class, the interviewees may be distrustful and question how their remarks will be used.

What is obvious is that when it comes to being negatively influenced by the media, African American women are no different from other ethnic groups, particularly since thinness is increasingly idealized. We aren't suggesting that there's anything wrong with women of any race being thin and beautiful, of course, as long as it doesn't require obsessive behavior to look that way. The message for all parents is that we can teach our daughters that loving their bodies as they are naturally corresponds with healthy, not obsessive, eating and exercising.

(54) Think Long and Hard Before Sending
Her to a Weight Camp

Most parents whose daughters struggle with obesity have noticed the ads for summer camps that promise to slim down overweight children. If you're considering sending your daughter to a so-called fat camp, you should be aware that if you don't handle the matter carefully, your daughter could begin to view herself as the family member who has the "problem" body that needs to be "fixed."

If you are considering a weight camp, remember that most usually have high rates of recidivism. So in addition to asking about their techniques, it's important that you thoroughly question the administrators of the camps you are considering about their success rates. Inquire also about postcamp programs for sustaining the progress.

Children tend to lose weight while enrolled in these summer camps, and when they return home, they receive lots of positive attention about their success. But by Thanksgiving, many have regained the weight they lost, as well as a few extra pounds. Setbacks like this make them feel even more defeated about their bodies. Also, children who are sent away to these camps sometimes feel abandoned by their parents and believe they're being punished for being overweight.

Should you opt for one of the camps, explain to your girl that her body is not a "problem" and that her experience will help the whole family create an environment that is more conducive to a healthy lifestyle for everyone. One young woman returned from camp asking that her mother serve less red meat and cheese. At previous meals the family had been consuming high-calorie foods such as steaks, chops, roasts, pizza, and macaroni and cheese. The entire family felt better when they cut excessive fat and cholesterol from their diets.

Finally, don't forget to consider the benefits of weight camps, too. Surrounded by children with similar issues, your daughter may be more likely to participate in activities and sports that she has shied away from in the past because she feared that she couldn't keep up with other children or that she might be teased. She may also feel accepted by her campmates in ways she has not recently experienced. After considering the advantages and disadvantages, make an informed decision that, above all, helps your daughter see her body as a beautiful work in progress.

(55) Cut Out or Obscure Size Labels in Her Clothing

It's so easy to get hung up over sizes. You may have spent a great deal of energy in your own life wishing you were a smaller size. There's no reason to pass this misery on to your daughter. Her self-image shouldn't be tied to a number, which, by the way, varies according to the manufacturer.

Once she reaches puberty, if she moves up to a larger size for reasons unconnected to growing taller, you can take some of the focus off the size by cutting out clothing labels. You may also sew or iron leftover summer camp labels with your daughter's name over the size labels. That way, her clothes will say who she is, Laurie Smith, not "size fourteen." That's who she really is anyway. Ask your daughter to join you (or her dad, baby-sitter, or grandmother) in covering up or cutting out these labels. You may want to share some of your own experiences about how much energy you've wasted wishing you were a smaller size or how you've felt uncomfortable when you couldn't fit into a certain size. Assure your girl that as long as she maintains a healthy diet and engages in an active lifestyle, she will be the perfect size for her.

(56) Help Girls with "Perfect" Bodies Understand They're More than Just Pretty Faces

We've all heard the line "It's not easy being beautiful." It has to be a joke, right? After all, how could being "perfect looking" be a problem? In truth, beautiful girls can be vulnerable for much the same reason that some Hollywood beauties suffer. In a society in which the way we look counts for so much, some girls start to believe that they are nothing more than a body. They fail to develop the inner resources that are necessary for coping with life's disappointments.

It is also important to keep in mind the bitter irony that in a society in which physical perfection is so highly valued, perfect-looking women are often thought to be "stupid." Some perfect-looking girls become victims to this cruel stereotype and begin to view themselves as too "stupid" to learn.

Girls who give in to pressure from others to focus on their looks can be terrified about losing them. They realize, of course, that perfection is subject to fads and fashion. And because their power is tied to something that, by definition, will fade, they worry about what will happen when they become less than perfect. For much the same reason, the love they experience feels provisional. Just as a rich individual may doubt the motives of anyone who professes love, perfect-looking girls may question the love others extend to them. Their friendships can be affected by their looks, too. They sense the envy of other girls.

We have known young women who respond to looking "perfect" by caving in to societal pressure. They failed to develop inner selves and tied their esteem to their looks. If a boy spurns them, they feel it's because they aren't pretty enough. We also know a "perfect" girl who responded to the pressure by dressing herself in unattractive clothing and eating in an unhealthy manner. Fortunately, we can also say that we know a "perfect"-looking girl—so stunning that even at thirteen she could make you gasp—who has it all together. A photography enthusiast and a writer, Rita has developed a rich inner life. In fact, she seems to be lit from within.

If "perfect" looks is an issue for your daughter, you can help her create a balance in her life so she can actually see herself as beautiful through and through. The following are some suggestions:

- Teach her artfully to steer the subject away from her looks by saying something as simple as, "Would you like to hear me play my guitar?" Tell her this isn't bragging, but a polite way of saying that she's more than just a pretty face.

- Teach her to accept genuine compliments about her appearance with pleasure. Many "perfect"-looking women feel so burdened by their looks that they can't take joy in them.

- Since being beautiful is not enough to make her interesting or engaged in life, encourage her to develop interests that are uniquely her own. One woman whose daughter enjoyed reading about and listening to music by Judy Garland helped her girl get involved in a fan club dedicated to the star.

- If she watches television, point out commercials that feature athletes, celebrities, or children who others assume are not smart but who then make highly intelligent statements and stun others. Explain that these kinds of advertisements are popular because they're counterintuitive—not what people expect. Tell her that some missassumptions can be made to work to her advantage. If someone were to assume, for instance, that your daughter couldn't be smart because she's "perfect" looking, her highly developed intellect could be an extra-special gift for her. To that end, she might enjoy learning a new word a day, so she can create a stunning vocabulary. She might want to start by learning the word "counterintuitive."

(57) If She's Disabled, Teach Her to See Her Body as Beautiful

Some parents of disabled children try to avoid calling attention to their children's physical imperfections. They may think they're making it easier for their children, but silences and averted looks can communicate a message of shame, which the children internalize. Teaching our daughters to love their bodies means that they feel peace and acceptance for every aspect of their being.

That's something Toni Daniels, age forty-seven, learned early on. Toni contracted polio at age three, and from that point on, walking became difficult. Still, her mother, Loyce De Augustino-Todd, taught her to view her legs and feet as prized possessions. "From the time I was thirteen, my mom took me to get pedicures," Toni said. She was initially uncomfortable having strangers touch her feet, but learned to enjoy it. By the time Toni was an undergraduate at UCLA, her mom had persuaded her to add massages and manicures to her list of essential self-care practices. Toni believes that all of this gave her a heightened sense of who she is and a love for her entire body.

In addition to doling out special loving attention to the most deeply affected areas on your disabled daughter's body, you (or her dad, baby-sitter, or grandparent) can enhance her physical esteem by helping her make peace with the events that may have led to her disability. Any resentment that she may pick up on may lead her to view her body as a mistake.

In extolling the importance of forgiveness and closure, Toni, who is African American, tells of her childhood in Meridian, Mississippi, when she began suffering from a fever, headache, sore throat, and vomiting—symptoms that were familiar to many during this period, the height of America's polio scare. In 1952, more than 57,000 people were afflicted with the virus, which can attack nerve cells that control the muscles of the legs, arms, diaphragm, abdomen, and pelvis. Despite the spread of paralysis, Toni was refused treatment at a local hospital because they didn't admit "coloreds." Hours later, nurses at another hospital were about to send her away when a young white physician, recognizing that Toni was in respiratory arrest, insisted on treating her. By then, both her legs and her lower back were paralyzed.

Despite this loss, Toni said she is able to love her body because her family members never got caught up in blame and anger over her disability. "My relatives didn't say, 'This happened because mean white people turned you away. . . .' Instead they said, 'You are alive today because one person made a difference. You can also grow up and make a difference.'" That she has. In addition to an undergraduate degree, she earned a master's degree in business administration and, in 1991, was hired as the director of recruitment and admissions for the General Theological Seminary in Manhattan, a master's and doctoral-level Episcopalian institution. It's a job that requires her to travel thousands of miles a year and to deliver speeches that are rousing enough to draw students into the ministry. In an effort to present her best self, Toni has added a four-day-a-week gym workout to her health regimen.

Toni views her success as an outgrowth of her mother's efforts to convince her to love her body and her determination to find Toni a role model, someone who had encountered similar difficulties in life but who had made her own way. Toni suggests that the parents of disabled children do the same, contacting various agencies that work with special-needs populations and asking for suggestions of adults who may be willing to help change a child's life.

Toni's role model was also her baby-sitter: Wilma Rudolph. If that name sounds familiar to you, it may be because Rudolph was the first American woman to win three Olympic gold medals. Once called the "World's Fastest Woman," Rudolph had something in common with Toni. Until she was about twelve years old, Rudolph had been unable to walk without braces and orthopedic shoes, as a result of polio and scarlet fever. Toni's mother met Rudolph while teaching at Tennessee State University, which is located in the Olympian's home state.

Rudolph died in 1994—three days after Toni's mother did. Looking back on their lives, Toni said that she learned from both women that when it comes to winning and losing, what is most important is focusing on one's inner strengths. Rudolph said of her 1960 Olympic victory in Rome: "It takes steady nerves and being a fighter to stay out there. . . . I could only hear the cheers after the race was over."[6]

VIII

Emotional Force

What She Feels Determines How She Treats Her Body

One of the most effective ways to bolster your daughter's body esteem is to help her develop her emotional intelligence. An awareness of her emotional life can determine how she cares for her body, how she evaluates it, whether she insists that others treat it respectfully, and even whether her body will cooperate as she pursues her dreams. In short, her future success will be determined by whether her mind and body are in conflict or attuned.

(58) Teach Her the Connection Between the Mind and Body

We have entered an era in which scientific studies have validated that the mind and body are interconnected and interdependent. Since the nervous system connects every cell of the body to the mind, body discomforts, and even diseases, can be influenced by conscious and unconscious thoughts and feelings. For instance, your daughter may get upset about something she hears and may throw up. Her nausea may have been induced by a brain chemical.[1] Or perhaps you know a girl who gets nervous and breaks out in hives. These unsightly splotches may occur because her sympathetic nervous system (which controls physical responses to emotions) went into overdrive and sent blood rushing into her vessels.[2]

Understanding the mind's connection to the body doesn't necessarily mean never experiencing discomfort. Also, sometimes a headache is just a headache. And when considering any serious ailment, you must, of course, take genetic and environmental factors into account. Still, it is important to teach your girl how to assume an active role in managing and understanding her health through a combination of conventional treatment and mind-body approaches. Your daughter will feel empowered if she is involved in her own self-care, identifying emotions that she may have unconsciously ignored.

Perhaps your daughter has struggled with an ailment, such as stomachaches or recurrent colds. In addition to consulting a physician, encourage her to listen to her "internal dialogue" and interpret the message behind her symptoms. Journal writing is one of the most effective means of exploring an "internal dialogue." Ask her to fold a page into four columns. In the far left-hand column, your daughter can record her physical symptom. In the next column, ask her to record what might have been happening to cause the upset in her body: perhaps a friend snubbing her at lunch or a bully's cruel taunts. (Explain that if her physical discomforts are connected to feeling upset, it doesn't mean that her pain is imaginary.) In the next column, she can record "What I did." She may write, for instance, "I laughed along with the other kids so they wouldn't know I was hurt." Or she may say, "I cried." In the final column, the one farthest to the right, tell her to record what she wanted to say. She may write, "You idiot! I wish the teacher had left you back." Though your daughter will not feel "instant" relief, she will feel she's taking charge of her emotional and physical health.

Few girls understand the power of the mind-body connection better than Elane's fifteen-year-old daughter, Danielle, who—as we mentioned in the Introduction—was diagnosed with AML (acute myeloid leukemia) a highly aggressive form of leukemia. While her physicians and her family did everything within their power to help (her brother Deren donated his marrow to her, a painful procedure for him), Danielle used the force of her mind and body to fight for her own life. The following is an amalgam of some of her journal entries.

> All of this started with me getting colds that went away, and my family thought that was just normal. Then it got worse. I was tired a lot and knew something was wrong. I went to the doctor, then the emergency room and was diagnosed with leukemia. I was scared because I realized I might die. But I've been scared before. I play soccer, I'm a forward, and I know that no matter how bad things might look, if you can fight your way through, there's always light at the end of the tunnel. I knew cancer could slow me down, but that I could overcome it.
>
> It's not enough to just have a positive attitude. I didn't pretend that everything was all right. I was angry sometimes, sad sometimes, and I cried, and I can't believe it, sometimes, a lot of the time, I was even very happy. My music meant so much to me, and so did what I'd learned in temple about God never leaving

me. And I couldn't have done this without my family, friends, and the support of kids from my school.

The chemotherapy was bad, but the transplant was horrible. It felt like the chemicals and radiation were destroying my body, but I knew they couldn't penetrate deep enough to touch my spirit.

And you know what? Now that I'm better, I know what people mean when they say there's light at the end of the tunnel. The light is life! Although cancer was by far the scariest thing I have ever been through, I am grateful for it. I wake up mornings with a newfound appreciation and gratitude for the life flooding through me. Sometimes, during the course of my day, I pause and step out of my body and watch myself live every moment. I am so grateful for the blessing that is my life.

Danielle thinks it's important to remind kids that survival isn't always a triumph of mind over matter. While hospitalized, she developed a relationship with a girl who also expressed her deepest feelings and who received love and support from others, yet this girl lost her life to cancer. Danielle realizes that while establishing a mind-body connection doesn't always mean winning, an individual's body is more likely to respond to treatment when the person is emotionally and spiritually engaged in the fight.

Feeling empowered by her victory, Danielle has launched the Danielle Teen Foundation and is distributing "care packages"— which include body lotions, powders, and fragrances—to teenagers who are hospitalized with life-threatening illnesses. She is concentrating on teenagers, she says, because while hospitalized, she realized just how different she was emotionally from younger cancer patients. Adolescents generally think of themselves as immortal but when faced with a life-threatening disease, their ability to think abstractly allows them to imagine their own deaths; which can lead to paralyzing depression. "I feel that depression is more deadly than the cancer itself because it makes the body weak and vulnerable," Danielle explained. Soon after she launched her organization, Danielle received contributions and many offers of help from young people and adults alike, as well as the support of a local hospital.

If you're interested in giving your daughter a rudimentary understanding of the connection between the mind and body, pick up a copy of *You Can Heal Your Life*, by Louise L. Hay. This classic book includes an easy-to-follow chart of symptoms and the emotions that may be connected to them.

(59) Teach Her Some Anger-Release Exercises

Whether they are furious with you or a sibling or classmate or teacher, our girls need to know how to move the anger out of their bodies. Anger is a potent emotion that can build up in one's body, causing misbehavior, a loss of concentration, and ailments.

One anger exercise that can be used away from home involves writing angry retorts—for her eyes only—on toilet paper or tissues. Your daughter can compose these notes in a bathroom stall or anyplace where she can have temporary privacy. A note may say something along the lines of "Amy, this is what I wanted to tell you after you put that 'kick me' note on the back of my pants. . . ." Point out to your girl that since no one else will read what she writes, she can let her anger rip.

It's interesting to watch girls who envision themselves as the sweetest, kindest beings (and that may well be true) get in touch with the power of their anger during these writing exercises. Some use swear words for the first time and even blush as they write down what they wish they had said. Explain to your daughter that one of the most important aspects of writing these notes is getting rid of them. She can imagine as she rips her paper into shreds that she's ripping into the person who angered her. Children also enjoy flushing away the scraps of paper and pretending their perceived enemies are being flushed away.

Girls age eight and younger enjoy working out angry feelings with soft-colored clay. Remember not to be judgmental if your daughter wants to share her angry feelings with you, especially if it's directed at you. Your supportive response will communicate that anger, properly expressed, can be empowering.

It's important for your daughter to know that anger is not a "bad" emotion; our survival depends on it. People get angry when they feel physically threatened, when their dignity is compromised, when they have been treated unfairly, have been insulted or demeaned, or when their goals have been thwarted.[3] Anger gives us opportunities to learn about hidden parts of ourselves and about our loved ones. Anger exercises are great because no one gets hurt, while the mind and body benefit from the release of strong emotions that may otherwise go underground.

When your daughter is at home, she can benefit from an effective parent-child anger exercise. With the daughter and parent sitting back to back, one person talks uninterrupted for three minutes, expressing whatever feelings she wishes. The other person may only say, "mm-hmm." If the other person stops talking before the three minutes are up, the other must remain silent until the full three minutes are up; then that person gets to talk. The two take turns until they have had their say. When finished, the two should talk together for at least five minutes, to allow for a sense of closure.

You may also want to hang a Velcro dartboard on your daughter's bedroom wall. It is great for times after she has vented her fury with you or another family member and needs time to move the anger from her body. Each time she hits the target with a Velcro ball, she can continue to express her anger. Exercises such as this can signal that you're raising your daughter in a home where there is room for a full range of emotions.

(60) Teach Her to Soothe Herself Before a Challenging Task

When they're young and feeling hurt or sad, our daughters can turn to us for comfort. But as they grow more independent, they need to know how to reach inside for the nurture and comfort they need during times of high stress, such as school presentations and when they experience hurtful encounters. In teaching our daughters to lower their own stress levels, we are communicating an important message: They already have within them what they need to relax their bodies. The following are a few suggestions:

- **Conscious breathing:** This is a perfect exercise for a school-age child because it's simple and doesn't require her to close her eyes or look away from the front of the classroom. Explain to your daughter that when she was upset as a baby, she responded by arching her back and holding her breath because that is what infants do, sometimes until they turn red in the face. As we grow older, although we learn to moderate this stress response, most of us unconsciously tighten our muscles and take rapid, shallow breaths. Offer to teach your daughter how to breathe in a way that will allow her to calm herself, think clearly, and look positively cool without anybody else being the wiser. Begin by explaining that although she will eventually be able to do this exercise while sitting and without moving her hands, she needs to start out standing, with a palm on her stomach. As she inhales, she can push her stomach out like an expanding balloon; when exhaling, her stomach should be pulled in. After a few minutes she will feel her body and mind relaxing.

- **Meditation:** She can do this exercise while sitting and with her eyes open, but if she's in school, your daughter will have to select a time when she can afford to look distracted, such as in study hall. Tell her to begin by relaxing through conscious breathing and then search the room for something attractive that she can focus on, such as a notebook on which she has affixed a favorite picture, a poster, a textbook, or a drawing. Tell her to begin by staring at this object and trying to think of nothing else. If noise or voices around her break through her thoughts, tell her to notice them and then bring her attention back to her focal point. As distracting thoughts or emotions surface, she can gently remind herself that, for the moment, nothing else except the selected image is important to her. As she continues, teach her to notice every detail in her focal point, seeing aspects that she may ordinarily ignore. She can continue this exercise for two to ten minutes. When she has finished, she will feel more peaceful.

- **Visualization:** Since even adults are terrified at the thought of having to make speeches or presentations in their own fields of expertise, it's a given that our children will not be overjoyed with assignments that require them to address the class or school assembly. At least when adults speak, we can expect members of the audience to be receptive and polite, but obviously that's not a given in the classroom.

Once your daughter learns to use the power of visualization, she can handle these situations with aplomb. Here's how it works: In the week leading up to her presentation, in addition to thoroughly researching and preparing her project, she can spend a few minutes a day sitting or stretched out in a room where she will not be distracted. With her eyes closed, she can relax her body through conscious breathing and see herself calmly and thoroughly researching and studying her information.

As she continues breathing consciously, tell her to envision herself filling with the light of knowledge. This light continues to glow around her—just as the stars of the show *Touched by an Angel* radiate light—as she opens the door to her classroom, walks to the front, and begins her presentation. Looking out from the front of the class, she sees that the information is filling everyone present with a similar glow. Even the class clown is filled with this light. She can also see how comfortable she looks in her body as she speaks. As this visualization concludes, she hears her classmates cheering. As the cheers grow louder, she can open her eyes. Tell her to keep practicing this exercise in the days leading up to the presentation.

(61) Nurture Her Sense of Humor

Laughter can help your daughter ease the tension in her body and make her feel more optimistic about her immediate future. Author Laura Day explains, "When we laugh our body produces the same kind of chemicals as when we have a massage, dance, or do other pleasure-producing activities."[4] Humor is also a coping therapy that can help people survive difficult times. With all the drama that accompanies adolescence, it can certainly be helpful if you and your daughter can laugh at life's absurdities.

When it comes to the direction your daughter's laughter takes, you should know that children tend to follow their parents' leads. In some households, family members tend to laugh because they are making fun of others. Laughter at someone else's expense is never channeled from the spirit within, so it doesn't improve moods. There are ways to encourage spirited laughter, however. Here are some suggestions:

- Encourage the entire family to visit a local karaoke club and to perform. You will laugh at yourselves as you sing your hearts out.

- Host a family Olympics night, with parents competing against children in physical feats that are selected by the children. Categories might include everything from rollerblading to tricycle riding to cartwheels. Don't forget to invite grandparents.

- Read aloud children's poetry and books. Some of the most amusing poets include Roald Dahl, Shel Silverstein, and Jack Prelutsky. Don't forget stories by PBS humorist Daniel Pinkwater, including his *Space Aliens with a Yen for Junkfood* and *Frankenbagel Monster*. Also, check out books by author and illustrator James Stevenson, including his classic, *Are We*

Almost There? Families who enjoy Afrocentric picture books will be amused by *Leola and the Honeybears,* by Melodye Rosales; *Raising Dragons,* by Jerdine Nolen; and *What a Truly Cool World,* by Julius Lester.

- Teach girls, age fifteen and over, the concept that humor is sometimes a healthy response to sorrow. She may enjoy watching the film *Life Is Beautiful* with you.

- See a performance of Cirque de Soleil. In this touching, intelligent, and funny circus, performers achieve the "impossible" with their bodies. And don't forget the Bard. Shakespeare's *The Taming of the Shrew,* for instance, is hilarious. Before attending a performance, you may want to explain the plot to your daughter.

- Accompany children age ten and older to art houses to see films by Charlie Chaplin, the Marx Brothers, Buster Keaton, and W. C. Fields. Their comedic talents are gifts from the past that should be shared.

- Rent and watch together a video starring Robin Williams, such as Disney's *Aladdin* (Williams is the voice of the genie), *Mrs. Doubtfire,* or any Muppets film. Your children may have seen them, but they'll enjoy sharing a laugh with the family gathered together. You may also want to introduce children age thirteen and older to *Tootsie,* in which Dustin Hoffman plays a character who disguises himself as a woman. This film makes a great conversation starter about the feminine body and how others perceive it. Other humorous titles include: *Waking Ned Devine* and *The Gods Must Be Crazy.*

(62) Let Her Cry It Out

When our children are infants, they train us to rush to their aid as soon as we hear their cries or see their tears. That's what's supposed to happen. Research indicates that parents who pick up infants when they cry during the first year have babies who are less fussy later in life. As toddlers continue to communicate their unhappiness with their tears, it actually comforts us to comfort them. Lifting our little ones, we cradle their heads in the napes of our necks, and they wrap their legs around our hips. These treasured moments are something we miss once our children grow older.

So it's perfectly natural that when our children grow into adolescence and are much too big for us to lift anymore, we still want to wrap our arms around them and stem their tears. But there's a good reason not to give in to that temptation.

The older our children get, the less they cry, and crying can actually be good for them. Crying produces relaxation chemicals that can positively alter the body's biochemistry by assisting in the release of toxins and lowering tension levels. That's one reason people often feel better after a "good cry."[5]

Admittedly, trying to stop yourself from rushing to your daughter's aid is no easy feat, but holding back will give her an opportunity to experience her feelings. Then after a few minutes, rather than promise, "It will be all right," just hold her and be there for her. Try murmuring words such as, "That's too bad" or "What a bummer."

You should also hold back if she runs to her room and slams the door. Let her be for a while. It really is OK for her to stay with her sad feelings as she learns to soothe herself. A few minutes later, you get to give her the affirming messages she needs to hear—that you are there for her and want to support her. This way, you will have signaled that you're comfortable with a full range of her emotions. Her body will be all the healthier for it.

(63) Honor Her Friendships

What do friendships have to do with emotional stress and its affect on your girl's body? Plenty, as it turns out. Scientists have long recognized that humans respond to stress by preparing for battle or fleeing—the so-called fight-or-flight syndrome. But new findings suggest that females may show a different response to stress. According to a study led by Dr. Shelly E. Taylor, professor of psychology at the University of California, Los Angeles, girls and women may react to stress by seeking support and nurturing others rather than becoming aggressive or escaping.[6]

The results of this research are still preliminary. But parents who have seen a stressed-out young daughter soothe herself by singing a lullaby to a doll or have seen a teenage girl slam a door one minute and then get on the phone and laugh and joke with a friend the next will know there has to be some truth to the study.

Whom your daughter befriends is another body issue. As adolescents begin to pull away from their parents, they often turn to their friends for advice on topics like sex and the use of drugs and alcohol. Obviously, the more grounded and healthy your daughter's friends are, the more likely she is to get sound advice from them. And though you can't pick your daughter's friends for her, when she's ten or younger you can steer her toward girls whose families have values that are similar to yours. Once you steer her in the right direction, however, trust her instincts about whom she wants to spend time with.

By the time your daughter reaches middle-school age, there is a chance that some of her early friendships will remain intact. Some girls also maintain good friendships with boys. These platonic relationships can be valuable alliances. Boys often offer girls who are their friends important information about how to maintain their integrity around other guys. Also, take heart if your daughter isn't part of the "in" crowd. "Popular" girls are often the ones who have conformed to cultural directives about how a girl should view her body.

You can also support your daughter's need for friendships by modeling for her the importance of these relationships. If she sees you making an effort to maintain connections with friends despite the fullness of your life, she will respect her own need for friendships. You can also strive to make your home a place where other girls can congregate and enjoy privacy.

If your girl tends to be the independent loner type, and many strong girls are, try to interest her in activities in which she can meet other girls of like mind, such as a summer specialty camp or at an extracurricular activity. If you have moved with your daughter to a new neighborhood, and she left good friendships behind, let her know you understand her losses and encourage her to form new relationships. Finally, since some girls don't feel the need for a special friend as much as they need to feel included and cared for by a group of girls, support her involvement in programs such as the Girl Scouts or Campfire Girls.

(64) Teach Her to "Read" Her Photos

Photoanalysis, the psychological study of photographs, can be the basis for a meaningful and fun activity with your girl, one that can help her understand how her emotions can be seen in her body. The idea that photos, much like one's handwriting and dreams, can offer clues to the unconscious originated with Dr. Robert U. Akert. In his latest book, *Photolanguage: How Photos Reveal the Fascinating Stories of Our Lives and Relationships,* Akert explains that photographs are "like mirrors with memory." Once you and your daughter begin looking at photographs from the standpoint of how she was feeling in her body at a particular time, you'll never view one of her photos in the same way again. You can turn sharing photos with your daughter into a game. Wrap your head in a towel, add hoop earrings, and just like that, you've become Madam Zenobia, ready to read her photos. Here's how:

1. **Do advance work:** Gather a series of candid full-body shots that represent your daughter over a sweep of time.

2. **Invite your girl to join you:** Fan photos out like playing cards and ask her to choose one and tell you what she can remember about the day it was taken and how

she was feeling. If she can't remember, fill her in on what you may recall about the experience.

3. **Explain why you're studying the photos:** Emotions can go so deeply "underground" that an individual sometimes has no idea how she's feeling. But since the body never lies, emotions are often conveyed in one's body language. Tell her you want to help her read what her body is saying, so she can develop an awareness of her authentic feelings.

4. **Teach her to read her photo/body language:** Consider whether she looks relaxed or tense. What do her facial expressions convey? Find one in which she is smiling; then cover her mouth and examine her eyes. Do her eyes look joyful? Do they contradict what her smile is saying? Is there a shot in which she looks proud of her body or in which she's trying to conceal part of her body (out of shame, perhaps)? How about one in which she looks as if she feels completely accepted and loved or in which she seems to separate herself from others (with space, jutting elbows, or tilting her head away)? Are her hands balled into angry fists or are they relaxed? Share your observations with her.

5. **Give her a vocabulary to describe her emotions:** Explain that there are no bad emotions. But when experiences make us feel uncomfortable, we may feel numb, angry, sad, frightened, hateful, lonely, hurt, bored, betrayed, frustrated, inferior, repulsed, shy, confused, rejected, unfulfilled, weak, guilty, shameful, or empty. When we feel great, we may experience a sense of triumph, hope, self-confidence, affection, joy, love, belonging, relief, contentment, equality, trust, attraction, curiosity, clarity, support, satisfaction, strength, inno-

cence, pride, and contentment.[7] All of these emotions can be conveyed through body language.

6. **Identify a photo in which she is trying to conceal her feelings:** Ask her to comment on what she sees expressed in her body. Explore together why she felt she had to "cover up."

7. **Identify a photo in which she is expressing what she feels:** Explain that you want to support her so she can continue to feel this freedom in her body.

(65) Help Her Understand the Difference Between Emotional Eating and Healthy Eating

Despite all the talk about emotional eating—using food to fill an emptiness created by desperate needs—it's a difficult concept to grasp. After all, when your daughter was an infant and signaled her unhappiness with tears and cries, you often comforted her with food. Holidays tend to be celebrated with joyful eating, so she probably has body memories that link food and happiness. Nor is it unhealthy when someone occasionally cheers herself up with a food or beverage treat. So it's not surprising that your daughter may reach for a food that feels rich and rewarding when she's bored, sad, or tense.

So how do we know when our children cross the line and become obsessive overeaters? If your daughter weighs more than her physician deems healthy for her height and frame and her weight is not connected to a medical disorder, she is probably eating emotionally. But you don't have to wait for her to become overweight. Some emotional eaters don't put on weight until they reach puberty. So ask yourself whether your daughter regularly uses food as a mood enhancer. For example, does she overeat when she returns to an empty house after school and feels lonely? (She may call it feeling "bored.") Or you may have noticed that around your house a lot of food—a bag of unopened chips, a box of cereal, a bag of cookies—seems to vanish into thin air. It's difficult for emotional eaters to stop at just a few pieces or bites. Maybe you've ruled out everyone else in the household but assume it can't be your daughter, because you seldom see her snack. But emotional eaters are more likely to eat secretly. You may find candy or other junk-food wrappings hidden in her room. We know of one young woman who used to throw the empty packages out her bedroom window into her backyard.

If emotional eating is a problem for your girl, you will be more of a help to her if you remember that this has nothing to do with discipline. She's eating to fill an unconscious need. The following are some specific suggestions for learning to eat in a manner that will leave her feeling emotionally and physically satisfied. (Be sure to consult her physician about any plans you or she may have to change her diet.)

- **Start a food diary:** Ask her to keep track of what she's eating in a small notebook for at least four days. Look over this list and discuss what she was feeling or experiencing when she made these food choices.

- **Create a healthy food plan:** Consider which foods need to be added, substituted, or eliminated to create a healthy eating plan.

- **Make the connection:** If she finds herself unable to follow her eating plan, teach her to make the connection between her emotions and what she's overeating. For instance, did her teacher say something to embarrass her in class? She may have responded by eating an extra dessert at lunchtime. When she is able to connect the overeating with specific experiences, a pattern will emerge. When we recognize a pattern, it is called a flashpoint. These moments of intense light can help her understand the need she's trying to satisfy with food. Encourage her to talk about these feelings and try to come up with some strategies that can change what she does when she's in a situation in which she usually overeats.

- **Discuss why the extra food can't improve her life:** When the two of you are together, help her understand that the food only gives her temporary comfort because she can never fill a bottomless hole. If necessary, run water through a strainer and explain that the comfort food provides leaves her body in much the same way—it quickly runs out.

- **Identify the payoff:** Everyone who overeats has a secret pay-off, counsels Phillip McGraw from the *Oprah* show. Perhaps being overweight helps your daughter feel safer or closer to you (because, in your concern over her weight, the two of you spend a lot of time together—and she's now getting your attention, even if it is negative attention). Brenda's daughter, Carolyn, who had moved to a new city, overate at lunchtime and after school, because that's when she felt the loss of the friends in her old neighborhood—kids she had known since kindergarten. She overate to soothe herself and numb her grief.

- **Devise strategies:** As Dr. Phil further advises, it's important to plan what your daughter can give herself instead of food, when the hurtful feelings surface. Carolyn learned to reach out to new acquaintances, express her anger over the move, play her drums, E-mail old friends, and play basketball in a nearby gym. She also began to envision herself with a fitter, healthier body, and planned her meals in advance.

  If your daughter is eating to soothe the loneliness of returning home to an empty house, here are some possible strategies: Calling you at work; creating a "time bank"—a jar of notes that she writes about being alone, so the two of you can read and discuss these later; joining an after-school center, where she can get homework done as well as play with friends.

  Michelle Joy Levine, Ph.D., advises her clients to employ

delay strategies when they are about to eat something other than a normal meal or healthy snack. She suggests waiting ten minutes, which is actually only a short time for something so important.[8] Your girl might want to use that time to consider why she's about to binge and what set it off. And just as your hugs and kisses made her feel better when she was little, love can help now—only now she can learn to give herself what she needs. Encourage her to visualize her parents giving her a hug, saying, "We love you very much."

· **Help her remain aware of how much she's eating:** When possible, buy individual serving packages of snacks. Although these packages tend to be more expensive than larger ones, they can help emotional eaters keep track of normal portions. This is preferable to eating out of a large bag. For the same reason, using individual teaspoon-size sugar packets is preferable. At supper, individual plates can be filled from the stove, rather than from large bowls or platters of food on the table. This way, if an emotional eater wants to refill her plate, she has to get up and walk back to the stove, which will give her time to consider whether she actually needs more food. Finally, remember that watching television and eating at the same time is a bad idea, especially for emotional eaters, who tend to lose track of how much they're consuming while they're watching.

· **Don't scold or punish her if she slips up:** Reassure your girl that it takes time to learn to give herself the love she needs rather than punish her body with food. With your love and support, she will learn.

(66) Understand How Perfectionism and the Need to Please Are Linked to Eating Disorders

As with overeating, chronic undereating has been linked to emotional factors. Research has shown that having a poor body image is a significant predictor of future eating disorders. In the United States, an estimated one in six teenage girls has symptoms of eating disorders, such as bulimia or anorexia.[9] Millions more suffer from borderline variations, and untold millions more are unhealthy chronic dieters. It's a problem that can begin early in life. According to the Eating Disorders Awareness and Prevention (EDAP) campaign, 51 percent of nine- and ten-year-old girls report feeling better about themselves when they are dieting. EDAP further points out that among "normal dieters" 35 percent become pathological dieters, and of those, 20 to 25 percent will progress to partial or full-syndrome eating disorders.

Anorexia nervosa, in which individuals greatly restrict what they eat, to the point of poor health, can cause a girl to have irregular periods, dry skin and brittle hair, premature loss of bone density, and muscle atrophy.[10] People who suffer from bulimia eat large amounts of food in a short time and feel unable to control this bingeing. They use strategies to "reverse" the effects of their overeating, including self-induced vomiting, laxatives, diuretics, or excessive exercise.[11]

Whether it's anorexia or bulimia or other serious patterns of undereating, low weight and insufficient body fat can have serious implications, including the disruption of sex hormones, which can result in low estrogen levels. Since estrogen helps maintain bone density, girls with disordered eating patterns run the risk of stress fractures and are later prone to developing osteoporosis.[12]

If you have a daughter who has become obsessive about limiting her food intake, you should immediately seek medical and therapeutic intervention. If, however, your daughter is not diagnosed with an eating disorder, but you worry that she may eventually go that route, it may help to familiarize yourself with behaviors associated with disordered eating.

People with anorexia tend to be perfectionists.[13] In the same way that it may matter greatly to a perfectionist if she receives a 99 instead of 100 on an exam, only superthin, not just thin, will do. She may decide to eliminate fat from her diet, but if she "slips up" and eats chips, she may decide to compensate and do "better" by eating only tuna in water with lettuce. Eventually, she may cut out the tuna and eat only the lettuce.

Ty Yarnell, a licensed clinical social worker in Auburn, California, who specializes in children's issues, explains that perfectionism tends to be generational. For instance, if your daughter is a perfectionist, you may recall one of your parents struggling with anxiety disorder or depression. These issues are actually linked. People often feel anxious or depressed when they can't accomplish the impossibly high goals they set for themselves. Some people misunderstand perfectionism. It doesn't always mean a drive to be perfect in every way. Some perfectionists may be sloppy around the house, but be perfectionistic about work.

If you (or your daughter's father) had parents with these issues, consider whether either of you felt pressured by their unreasonably high expectations. If so, one of you may have passed this tendency on to your daughter. This doesn't mean that one of you may be at fault, but by examining your own past and your behaviors, you can help discourage "body perfectionism" in your daughter. Martin M. Antony, Ph.D., and Richard P. Swinson, M.D., the authors of *When Perfect Isn't Good Enough,* suggest several strategies for coping with perfectionism. We have revised two of these strategies to help you to discourage undereating patterns that may be driven by perfectionist thoughts.

- **Record perfectionist thoughts about food and challenge them in writing:** In a journal, your daughter can record thoughts such as, "I should weigh less." She can then write a rebuttal with a healthier alternative thought, such as, "It's OK for me to weigh what I do." Then teach her to critique both the perfectionistic and the alternative thoughts. For instance, "My expectation that I should weigh less makes me worry so much about my body that I can't concentrate on anything else" and "If I eat what I need to and remain active, I will reach a weight that's healthy for me." She can finish off her entry with a helpful perspective, such as, "Allowing myself to reach a healthy weight may not be easy for me, but I'm glad I'm learning to treat my body with love."

- **Experience most-feared situations:** This exposure strategy involves putting oneself in a fearful situation repeatedly until the fear has ceased. For example, if someone is fearful of eating a balanced meal but practices doing so despite initial discomfort, the fear will begin to ebb. Exposure works best if your daughter records her efforts. She can list the date and time that she eats a nutritious meal, add a few words about her situation (school cafeteria or dinner at home, for instance), and then rate her anxiety level on a scale of zero to ten. Over time, her anxiety about eating may abate.

There are also particular behaviors associated with bulimics. They give over much of themselves to others and unconsciously believe that food is the only comfort they provide for themselves. After excessive eating, they feel shame about their out-of-control behavior and attempt to impose order and control in their lives by purging.[14]

Even if there's little chance that your daughter will become bulimic, she can benefit from learning how to assert her will. The need to please others is a problem for many girls and women who believe they are being selfish if they don't place the needs of others above their own. But self-care is critical. One way to model it for our daughters is to let them hear us saying no to others. It's also important for them to see us taking care of our own needs.

That's one reason you should make plans around your own interests, such as a night out with friends. Your daughter should understand from your actions that you are taking time for yourself. You can further help her by encouraging her to practice how to decline requests from others without feeling she has to offer excuses. Tell her to stall for time if her courage fails her, and add that she can say that she will get back with an answer. This ploy will help her buy time and gather her inner resources, so she can say no with conviction.

(67) Enhance Her Emotional Intelligence

It's great when girls are encouraged to pursue intellectual interests and experience academic successes. But it's equally important to keep in mind that just as we should never encourage our daughters to focus only on appearance, we should not encourage them to rely purely on their intellectual skills while ignoring their feelings. Emotional health requires an integration of the whole person.

A girl who lives exclusively "in her head" may eschew physical workouts and spend all her extracurricular time preparing for the next big exam. She may find herself taking lots of sick days, never making the connection, for instance, between her spate of colds and the fact that her immune system has been compromised by nonstop stress.

What can you do if you are raising a girl who's "all in her head"? Point out that you may have discouraged her from expressing her feelings. Tell her a little bit about how you learned to be that way and discuss with her how you can both change. Then encourage her to use "I feel" statements. For instance, rather than say, "The science show was good," she might say, "I liked the fair because it was good to be around a lot of other kids who have the same interests as mine. Sometimes I feel very different from my classmates." Rather than "He's a lousy teacher," she might say, "That teacher makes me feel ashamed when I make a mistake." It takes some practice, but she can learn.

Also, use your daughter's ambitions to encourage change. Point out that the best colleges pursue students who use their bodies and minds in tandem—participating in sports, performing volunteer work, or honing special talents. Mention also Daniel Goleman's *Working with Emotional Intelligence*. In that book, Goleman concludes, from an analysis of 500 corporations and government and nonprofit agencies, that when it comes to success, emotional intelligence counts even more than intellectual intelligence or professional expertise.

IX

She Is Woman

Raising Girls to Feel Proud of Their Female Bodies

For thousands of years, cultures have used female biology as an excuse for confining girls and women to narrow roles. But as mothers today, we have the power to teach our girls to take joy in—not simply recognize—the capacities of their female bodies. In passing on a belief system that recognizes female strengths and identifies what it truly means to be in a womanly body, we can transform the possibilities of whom our daughters can become.

(68) Identify Any Ambivalence
You May Feel About Menstruation

Many of us have long regarded our menses as something we have to tolerate. That's unfortunate because passing on a sense of ambivalence about this natural process prevents our girls from developing a sense of awe about their bodies. Menstruation is so integral to being a female that hating one's menarche will make it difficult for your daughter to love becoming a woman. For this reason, it's important for you to question any negative views you may have.

You can begin by considering your mother's experiences and how they may have shaped what she taught you about your feminine body. Many of us had mothers who came of age during times that were particularly disheartening for women. From limited college and work opportunities to societal pressure to abandon their dreams and devote their lives to the care and comfort of their husbands and children, many women of our mothers' generation felt intense or covert frustration with their lives. Niravi Payne, an internationally recognized leader in mind-body fertility, believes that this frustration affected the way a significant number of mothers of baby boomers viewed themselves as women, their own bodies, and especially their reproductive functioning. Furthermore, she believes that some of those damaging messages were passed on to baby-boomer women. Consider your experiences in this regard.

In addition to attitudes that your mother may have passed on to you, keep in mind that you may have inherited society's negative views about menstruation. In *The Goddess Within*, Jennifer Barker Woolger and Roger J. Woolger point out that many of the derogatory phrases commonly used in reference to menstruation "reveal an attitude to the female body that would be regarded as profoundly pathological in any other culture but our own."[1] Social critics have long blamed patriarchal views for the distortions. Gloria Steinem has suggested that if men menstruated and women could not, rather than see this process as something shameful, men would brag about how long their periods lasted and how heavily they bled.

Today we have an opportunity to pass on to our daughters a sense of peace about their menses. Rather than teach them that menstruation is something they have to suffer through, we can reframe the notion so our girls can view it as the gift it is—though this doesn't rule out expressions of annoyance and anger. One way to reframe menstruation for your daughter is to tell her that in ancient Egypt farmers knew that when the Nile overflowed the riverbanks and flooded the land there would be much inconvenience, but that once the waters receded, the land would be nutrient rich and supportive of tremendous growth. Tell her that the relationship between her body and her period is fairly similar—that there can be some inconvenience, but that her cycle signals the release of enriching hormones that contribute to a look of health and vitality and signal the start of physical and creative growth.

If it's appropriate, you may want to add that when you were growing up, you were not taught about the gift of menses and that you want to pass on to her a sense of gratitude for this natural process. Explain that a lot of women don't realize how good menstruation is for their bodies until they stop getting their period each month.

Your daughter will also need to hear that menstruation is far more than a physical endowment; it also marks a time in her life when she can be tremendously creative. Toward this end, encourage her to do some journal writing, so she can strengthen the connection between her intellect and her burgeoning inner wisdom. Tell her that her period will enable her intuitive powers to soar. As biologist-psychologist Joan Borysenko explains, it is the pineal gland, buried deep within the brain, that communicates to the pituitary gland when it is time to begin secreting the hormones of puberty. Borysenko writes, "In Eastern cultures, the pineal corresponds with the sixth chakra, or third eye. So perhaps at puberty, when the output of hormones from the pineal is at its peak, we have a literal opening of that wisdom eye."[2]

Premenstrual stress syndrome is a subject that certainly calls for reframing—especially in light of television commercials that make women appear to be on the edge of madness when they are about to get their periods. Explain that because ignorance breeds prejudice, many people make jokes about women being "bitches" when they menstruate. Explain that although some girls do experience discomfort and irritability, it helps to remember that this is a time of heightened passion—a "period" when she can love more deeply and use her anger as an instrument for change. Just as the moon grows, becomes full, and then wanes before bursting to life again, each menstrual cycle marks renewed opportunities for her to reshape her life. Since her body is psychically and biologically recharged each month, she can infuse whatever field she ultimately chooses, from science to the arts to education to technology, with great intelligence and spirit.

While you may decide to create a first menses celebration, keep in mind that many girls are uncomfortable with having a lot of attention called to their bodies at this time in their lives. If this is the case with your daughter, rather than a ceremony, perhaps she will enjoy an evening with her parents or a sister. One mother took her daughter outside to gaze at the moon and, in honor of the girl's creative power, gave her a tin of colored pencils, saying that they were symbolic of the colorful life that lay ahead.

(69) Help Her Develop a Sense of Pride and Ownership About Her Breasts

In today's increasingly eroticized culture, even the youngest girls are bombarded with media images of so-called perfect breasts. Young girls have probably always checked beneath their shirts, wondering when their breasts would begin to grow—some terrified that their breasts would never become what they're hoping for, with others imagining them as twin impediments that would eventually mean no more horsing around with the guys. That anxiety has been further heightened by our culture's tolerance for viewing girls' bodies as sexual.

One response to this pressure is that adolescent girls are submitting to surgical procedures in the hope of attaining the ideal. Nationwide in 1992, 1,172 teenagers had their breasts augmented.[3] Then, of course, there are all those girls who would submit to the surgery if they afford it and if their parents would let them. "Would I? Oh my god, yes, I'd love my boobs to be bigger!" said Shelly, a giggling thirteen-year-old. Covering a mouth shining with retainers, she added, "It's like, why not give the guys something bigger to stare at?" To listen to Shelly is to feel the abiding power of boys and men in this society. For it is still the male gaze that dominates the way so many girls view their breasts and gives them the sense that this very private body part does not belong to them.

We can challenge that notion, so our daughters can take responsibility for the health of their breasts and eventually take pleasure in them, by initiating early conversations that help them critically view and question society's mammary fixation. Girls as young as age seven and eight can share thoughts on what it may be like to live in a country where women go bare breasted in public. You can explain that women in some indigenous cultures begin to feel uncomfortable with their bare breasts when outsiders come in and focus attention on them. Imagine together what it would be like if aliens came to the earth and stared at girls' ears, shocked that humans didn't conceal them.

Also, remember that familiarity breeds comfort, respect, and a sense of ownership. As your daughter's breasts develop, encourage her to stand before a mirror and observe and examine them. Dr. Susan Love, coauthor of *Dr. Susan Love's Breast Book,* believes that it's important to explain that these self-examinations that girls begin from early ages are not about checking for cancerous lumps. She writes, "Getting well acquainted with your breasts is important because it gives you a good, integrated sense of your body."[4] You can reinforce this message by letting your daughter know that you're caring for your own breasts with monthly self-exams and, if your physician recommends, yearly mammograms.

It can also help to engage her in a conversation about society's mammary fixation. You may want to tell her how some people felt it was unbecoming behavior by U.S. Soccer player Brandi Chastain when she pulled off her jersey to celebrate her team's victory in the 1999 World Cup finals. Chastain was wearing an athletic bra (not unlike the top of a two-piece swimsuit). Ask your daughter why she thinks some people responded as they did, when similar behavior obviously would not have caused a stir if Chastain had been a man.

Finally, try to cultivate your daughter's sense of humor about our society's mammary fixation. Explain that to many people, breasts are symbolic of the nurture and security that a mother gives her child. So tell her the next time she sees a boy ogling her breasts or someone else's, she should try to imagine him in diapers with a cartoon balloon over his head, shrieking, "I WANT MY MOMMY!"

(70) Introduce Her to Her Vagina

When we asked mothers about their vaginas, they seemed embarrassed, as if this was a topic to be whispered about. In fact, as Eve Ensler discovered when she interviewed more than two hundred women on the subject, vaginas have been shrouded in secrecy. Ensler compares this female body part to "the Bermuda Triangle" because "Nobody ever reports back from there."[5]

Ensler can be said to be responsible for bringing the vagina out of the dark. Her hugely successful play *The Vagina Monologues,* the winner of the 1997 Obie Award, has delighted thousands since it opened in an off-Broadway theater. The production seems to have the same affect on theatergoers that we hope you can have on your daughter, to make her glad she has a "you know what."

When people call to order tickets to Ensler's play, many mumble the title or refer to it as the "V Monologues," or simply "Monologues." But once they sit through the play, after more than an hour of not only hearing the word *vagina* but crying and laughing over this body part, many of these same people, mostly women, come away with a renewed sense of self. One middle-aged woman says she left the production feeling she had a jewel box between her legs. While waiting for a taxi, she stood next to a woman she'd never seen before and asked, "Aren't you glad we have vaginas!" The other woman embraced her.

You may find that your daughter, as a youngster, is quite taken with her vagina. Encourage her high regard by avoiding words such as "pee pee," or "wee wee." As puberty approaches, your daughter may develop a sense of shame about this most auspicious organ. It doesn't help that by now she may have seen magazine ads for "feminine" sprays and douches, which suggests that vaginas give off a bad odor that should be covered up with sweet-scented sprays.

You can help your daughter by initiating conversations about her vagina. Encourage her to take a mirror, crouch, and take a look at its intricate beauty. Ask her to draw a picture of it. If she's stumped, tell her that some women have drawn pictures of beautiful seashells or flowers as representations of their vaginas. Also, ask some of the same kinds of questions that Ensler asked in her interviews: If your vagina could wear clothes, what would it have on? If it could talk, what would it say? If it had an accent, what would it sound like? One fourteen-year-old girl answered in a French accent, "Ooh la la la la la!"

If you can't see the play, we encourage you to read a copy of *The Vagina Monologues* book, which includes the script. You may decide to share it with your older teenage daughter and discuss it with her.

Another way of maintaining the fun and exhilaration that grows from these conversations is to develop a signal for you and your daughter, to remind her that her body is wonderful. After she has finished participating in a sports event or performance of any kind, give her the "Vee" sign with your fingers. People will think you're signaling "Peace," or "Victory." True on both counts. Your daughter will have the peace of mind that comes with loving all her body and victory over societal shame. The Vee is also to remind her of "Vagina Power." Lifting your two fingers in silence has nothing to do with shame but, rather, politeness. You don't want to inspire a terrible sense of vagina envy among any men who may be in the crowd.

(71) Teach Her About the Wisdom of Her Body

Once the diapers come off, one of the earliest mother-daughter body conflicts often involves going to the bathroom. It can be hard to search for a bathroom when you're traveling on a busy freeway, for instance, or in the middle of listening to a sermon. So you might ask your girl, "Can you just hold it for a minute?" But this approach is a missed opportunity to teach her about the wisdom of her body. Consider how seldom we honor the needs of our own bodies.

For many of us, the only times we really listened to our bodies was during our pregnancies, when we had cravings and gave in to them. Most of us didn't realize that these cravings had anything to do with body wisdom. Now researchers are finding that all through our pregnancies, our cravings direct us toward much-needed nutrients. And bouts of morning sickness actually kept us from eating or retaining certain foods that might have damaged the fetus when major organ systems were developing.[6]

Too bad, then, that most of us stopped paying attention to our body's wisdom as soon as we gave birth. How about you? Do you respond to your body's signals for even something as simple as taking a bathroom break, or do you put it off until you no longer can? How about when you're talking to someone and the hair stands up on the back of your neck? Do you pay attention to what your body may be telling you? Or do you find yourself saying later, "How could I not have known better?" Another clue as to how well you're tuned in to your body's wisdom is your approach to food. Our bodies literally shout at us when we've eaten too much, but many of us ignore the signals anyway.

Ignoring the body's wisdom comes directly from having been taught from an early age that "good girls" place the needs of others before their own. (It would make sense that if everyone else's needs are paramount, we wouldn't respect our own.) That's why many of us pass on the "you're-just-going-to-have-to-hold-it" baton to our daughters. Fortunately, we are creating a different legacy for our girls.

When your daughter grows beyond the age when you have to accompany her to the loo, there are other ways you can support her in honoring her body's wisdom. For instance, don't get caught up in the struggle over how much clothing she should wear on cold days. If she insists that she doesn't need a jacket, but you're worried that she'll "freeze to death," remind yourself that on cold days, some people wear heavy coats while others are comfortable in shirtsleeves. Individuals respond differently to temperatures, and what feels like freezing to you doesn't necessarily feel the same to your daughter. Rather than worry, tuck a fold-up parka in her backpack, so she can pull it on if the weather takes a sudden dip. That way you can spend your last few minutes before she leaves exchanging hugs rather than engaging in a losing battle.

Food will provide another opportunity for you to support your daughter in honoring her body. Early in her life, explain that she's lucky to be able to tap into her body's wisdom and recognize when she's actually hungry. That means you won't make her clean her plate. As the years progress, you'll find that you have many other chances to state clearly, "Honey, I'm sure you're a better judge than I about what your body is telling you, and I want to respect that."

Although we start them off in small ways, our daughters can learn to tune in to their bodies' inner voice when it really counts. An older girl may be able to say to herself, "There's something about the vibes this guy is putting out that makes my skin crawl. I'm leaving." When she explains why she's home early, you'll know it was worth it all those years ago to have gotten up in the middle of whatever was claiming your attention to take your daughter to the bathroom.

(72) End Those "Pain of Labor" Stories

Sometimes even the most sensitive mother goes into great detail in front of her children about the pain she suffered giving birth to them. While it's certainly true that labor pains are no day at the races, you have to wonder what the secret message is in these stories: "It lasted for two days. I begged the doctor for drugs. I felt as if my body was being torn in two." If the point of these details is to say, "This is how much I love you," then you need to know that it is not what's coming across. Most girls who hear these stories simply wish that they had been born men so they wouldn't have to experience labor pains.

What we want to do, of course, is help our daughters feel real gratitude for the miracle their bodies can accommodate. So if you have already shared these labor details with your daughter, ask her how she felt when she heard them and apologize if she says you frightened her.

Whether you're correcting a labor story or sharing birth information for the first time, you can present the details in the most positive manner. First consider the details that were omitted from your daughter's birth story. Was her father jumping for joy? Did her grandparents ask you to hold the phone to her ear so they could tell her how much they loved her? Of course we want you to be truthful about that day, but tell her the whole story. "Yes, it hurt, and that's why I'm grateful that women have a greater tolerance for long-term pain than men. My favorite memory of that day is . . ."

Children love hearing positive birth stories. Every time you share the details, you are enabling your daughter to take pride in her femaleness. No matter how familiar the story, you'll notice that she hangs on every word and insists that you repeat favorite details: "Did Daddy really cry? How much did I weigh?" As she matures, you will, of course, continue to mark her birthday with parties and gifts, but while celebrations are certainly important, you can enrich her sense of self by underscoring the miracle of her birth.

One father told his daughter about love at "first move." He explained that he'd loved his girl from the first time he felt her move inside her mother. He said he realized how amazing a woman's body is, that it can house and feed and deliver a perfect, miniature human being. Another woman told her daughter, "We saw you inside of me on the ultrasound, and you were waving your arms like a conductor." Whatever story you choose to share, stress the fact that you were blessed to be able to shelter her within you and keep her safe until she was ready to move out into the world.

(73) Don't Make Her the Live-in Baby-Sitter

Sara was only seventeen, but she was so determined that she would never become a mother that she refused to date, even when she was asked out by a boy she liked. The eldest of six children, Sara had spent much of her life "helping out" with the others, five days a week after school. When her mother asked why she'd refused a date to the prom, Sara said that since her grandmother had given birth to thirteen children and her mother to six, it was obvious that women in her family could get pregnant just by sitting beside a guy. Her mother laughed, not realizing the gravity of her daughter's words and behavior. Sara's mother didn't realize that Sara's life of child care had damaged her relationship with her body. Sara viewed women as "baby-making machines" who could be forced into lives of servitude because of their sex.

Although her views are extreme, Sara's situation certainly isn't. Young people like Sara are called "parentified" kids because they serve as stand-in parents, and they are often angry. Now that working mothers are the societal norm, older children are increasingly being relied upon to help raise their siblings. In healthy families, everyone is expected to pitch in and help out, but in some families, in which the parents are overburdened, an elder child—often a girl—is expected to step in and take over. Women who choose to become mothers may see child rearing as an honor and a blessing. Girls who are forced to take over child-rearing duties and become "little mothers" are often resentful of their responsibilities and of having been chosen for the work because of their sex.

There are also other emotional ramifications to consider. Since the parents are so busy, the child can lose her connection with them and feel abandoned. And because of her domestic responsibilities, she may not have time for friends or simply to be a child. Making matters even more difficult, younger siblings in her care are also angry over their parents' absence and often take their anger out on the sibling in charge.

If you are a working parent who relies on your daughter for baby-sitting help, try to broach the subject with her. She's sure to have a lot to say, and it's important that you hear her out. You should apologize for having to put her in that position. Even if you feel you had no other choice or she is unable to recognize how she feels, don't let yourself off the hook. Brainstorm with her about how you can create change in your lives.

(74) Surround Her with Vibrant Older Women

From an early age, we are haunted by the image of a frail and decrepit woman, stooped over and shuffling by. She haunts our consciousness because she is perhaps our greatest fear. Meanwhile, men are presented in the popular imagination as "studs to the end." It's a fairly absurd picture when you stop to remember that women tend to live longer than men do and that thanks to the advances of modern medicine there are many rigorous, fit, healthy older (not old) adults who are living life to the fullest.

Unfortunately, few children have the opportunity to rub shoulders with these older adults. In generations past, girls were exposed to a range of older women, such as grandmothers, aunts, and neighbors who were still active well into their eighties, as well as those who were infirm. Individuals were often born, raised, educated, and married in the same neighborhoods, remaining close to family members, including those who were aged.

Today there is more of a tendency for the oldest generations to be segregated from the daily lives of their extended families. As a result, our daughters often have little contact with older women. That's a real shame, not just because these women have wisdom to share, but also because the internalized popular image can lead girls to view their bodies as something they'll use up for the short term, rather than nurture for the long term.

You can help your daughter correct this misguided image of what she will eventually become. Start by doing something as simple as calling some of these women to your daughter's attention, perhaps taking her along to your health club. As these older, body-confident women mix with others of various ages and sizes—in locker rooms, Jazzercise classes, and weight rooms—they will become a natural part of her consciousness.

Tell her also about women such as Lindy Boggs, who at the time of this writing was the U.S. ambassador to the Vatican.

At eighty-five, Boggs, the mother of Washington journalist Cokie Roberts and the widow of Congressman Hale Boggs, is hard to keep up with. She works twelve- to fourteen-hour-days.[7] And these days, it seems everyone is familiar with glamorous Eartha Kitt, the seventy-three-year-old actress, singer, and dancer who can be spotted in Gap commercials or news segments as she stretches her flexible body in a yoga routine.

Just as important, encourage your girl to visit and develop a relationship with a vigorous older woman. You'll provide her with another rationale for taking care of herself. She'll begin to see her body as something that requires a long-term investment.

(75) Don't Let Your Gender Biases Constrain Healthy Behaviors

In too many homes, parents who are fearful of homosexuality discourage behaviors in their daughters that are not stereotypically feminine. Parents may insist, for instance, that a girl let her hair grow long or play with dolls rather than a truck, or take ballet instead of play softball. But if we are to teach our girls to love their bodies, we must encourage a range of behaviors that feel natural to them. If a girl happens to prefer behaviors that are not in keeping with her family's vision of femininity and her parents make her feel shame about who she is, she may end up feeling uncomfortable with her feminine body.

Although a girl's choices of play and clothing preferences have nothing to do with sexual orientation, it would be difficult to convince some parents of that. Psychologist April Martin, Ph.D., has worked with adults who carry chronic low-level trauma from having been raised with a barrage of messages that say "You aren't feminine enough."

Martin says that parents who force their daughters to behave within narrow feminine standards may do so out of the mistaken belief that they can influence a child's sexual orientation. But there's nothing a parent or anyone can do to influence a child's sexual orientation. Martin adds, "We don't know if homosexuality is genetic, or a result of brain chemistry or environmental influences. But we do know it's elemental to one's nature. If parents force the issue, they might get external compliance, but internally the child is at war with herself."

The lesson we can derive from this is that it's important that you support your daughter in behaviors that allow her to express her personality. These behaviors may include everything from climbing trees to participating in the local "all-boys" baseball team. And lose the word "tomboy," which has negative connotations. Try the term "athletic girl" instead. Finally, if your daughter is thirteen or older, you can initiate a conversation about what it means to be feminine by reading together and discussing *To Kill a Mockingbird*, by Harper Lee. The young narrator, who goes by the name "Scout," struggles with the question of what it means to act like a "lady."

(76) Encourage Her to Get Her Hands Dirty

The idea of encouraging a girl to go out and play in the mud may sound positively subversive to some parents. Although parents may be perfectly comfortable with their sons returning from the yard with their faces smeared with dirt, they want their girls to look like perfect dolls. But we believe that a girl who gets her hands dirty and is allowed to interact with, rather than feel intimidated by, her environment will grow up feeling unconstrained in her body, whether she's inside or out of doors.

We have noticed that some girls reach adolescence and seem to be only partially in this world. We call them girly-girls—as if they're girls twice over—because they haven't been encouraged to nurture the many aspects of their male and female selves. Survival in this world, like peace in the body, requires an internal balance of traits that are considered both feminine and masculine—so that a girl can be ferocious as well as nurturing, analytical as well as creative, contemplative as well as forthright.

So when it comes to endeavors that require inner resources,

girly-girls often lack passion and commitment. Even when they have innate talent, on an athletic field, for instance, they may show up to be seen, not to play. Ignoring the game, these girls do cartwheels or sing the lyrics of a favorite song. There's nothing wrong with singing or, for that matter, looking clean and neat and fashionable. But because girly-girls have learned to concentrate on the external, on how others perceive them, rather than have an inner sense of their own uniqueness, they often believe that they are "nothing" without the attention of others.

On the contrary, a grounded girl, having had the literal symbolic experience of playing in the mud, seems determined to experience the world. Are grounded girls less vain? Not judging from the bathroom cabinets of some we have known. These girls' shelves seem to groan from the weight of curling irons, tooth whiteners, acne creams, and all varieties of hair conditioners. But there may also be lice shampoo. They never know where life will take them.

Grounded girls do get caught in the storms of adolescence but seem to weather them better. And while many girls are chatterboxes from time to time, as bioenergetic analyst Dr. John Conger explains, "a grounded person need not speak to be heard while an ungrounded person may talk endlessly without result. . . . Being grounded is the prerequisite for feeling centered and being fully in contact."[8]

Sixteen-year-old Karen is a classic example of a grounded girl. Rather than coast on her good looks, she maintains excellent grades, enjoys playing the violin, and is wild about horses. Most evenings she can be found in her grandmother's barn, grooming and feeding her horse and cleaning out his stall.

On the weekends, Karen is often involved in riding competitions that include cross-country racing, jumps, and dressage routines. When asked why she is willing to dedicate so much of her time to the sport, Karen doesn't hesitate. "I love bonding with the horse. Some people assume it's about me controlling such a large animal, but you don't really control a horse, not if you want to win. It's about fitting your body into his and being able to sense what he's thinking, what he needs, so he can do what he has to. I have to be fully in control of my own body for the relationship to work." Karen is a reminder of an essential aspect of grounded girls: They feel at home in their bodies.

(77) Take Her for a Rain Walk

The next time it rains, invite your daughter to join you (or her dad, sibling, or grandparent) for a walk. Since many people unconsciously believe that girls are fragile, when the weather turns unpleasant they encourage their daughters to stay indoors. Point out to your daughter that her body can handle climate extremes. Tell her that exposure to different physical conditions will only make her body feel more alive and help her to understand just how adaptable her body is. As you walk arm in arm, take time to notice how different the environment seems when it rains, as if the world is being washed new. Enjoy stretches of silence as you feel the wetness on your cheeks and listen to the rain falling.

When the mood feels right, explain that walking together in the rain (as opposed to the sunshine) is symbolic of the rain that sometimes falls in a person's life. Obviously, there will be times when your daughter will face difficult situations when you're not around. Tell her that you want her to be able to look back and remember these times of physical closeness, because the body carries memories. You are giving her a gift, a message that she is a survivor, when you encourage her to associate comforting memories with inclement weather.

(78) Encourage Her to Learn to Swim

Knowing how to swim is great for girls, and not simply because it's a low-impact aerobic workout that exercises the lower and upper body. Just as important, perhaps, is the fact that swimming will allow her to move freely in the earth's waters, which have a special connection to the feminine body. After all, the fluids of Mother Earth's waters have the same components as the amniotic fluid that sustained her within you, and you within your mother, and her mother before her, and that one day may fill her womb as well. Also, as Christiane Northrup, M.D., author *of Women's Bodies, Women's Wisdom,* explains, there is a rhythmic connection between our menstrual cycle and the cycles of nature, including the ocean's ebb and flow.[9]

Swimming, particularly in an ocean, will give your daughter a sense of control over one of nature's most powerful forces. It will make her feel as if the world is full of limitless possibilities. Swimming also offers a particular advantage when it comes to body acceptance. This is one of the few sports in which participants wear clothing that reveals their true bodies. It will help your daughter to realize that hers is just one of many shapes and sizes. Unlike gymnastics, ballet, basketball, or any number of other activities, swimming doesn't require any single body type. Successful swimmers come in all sizes—tall, short, heavy-set, slim, and petite, as well as those who are physically challenged. Explain to your daughter that becoming a member of a swim team (or any team) doesn't necessarily mean she has to be the best or the fastest participant. It's important that you support your daughter's participation in activities purely for the sake of pleasure, something few of us have learned ourselves.

(79) Support Her in Caring for All Her Skin

Tactile studies that compare the sexes in skin sensitivity have found that females have greater skin sensitivity than males and a heightened sense of smell.[10] There is no better way to help our daughters celebrate their sensual acuity than to encourage bath rituals.

Skin care for most young people generally means remembering to apply sun block. But bath-time indulgences are a great way to lower stress levels and teach our daughters to care for all their skin—including the parts that are usually kept under wraps much of the day. Learning to feel comfortable with touching and exploring one's body is another important benefit of all-over skin care. This kind of familiarity can pave the way for the adult years when they will feel quite natural giving themselves monthly breast exams and enjoying adult touch. Plus, with the great variety of lotions and bath preparations available today, our girls can certainly have fun in the shower. The following are a few suggestions for soaking, lathering up, and smoothing down:

- **Create a bath-time tension reliever:** Have her drizzle a few drops of an aromatic oil on a hot, wet washcloth, close her eyes, and place it over her face for a few seconds.

- **Keep shower supplies within reach:** Once your daughter begins showering, hang a basket of scented shower gels and shampoos within easy reach. With their aromatic scents and soothing feel, these products require no more time than using a bar of soap, but they can quickly make her feel indulged and self-cared for. Tell her to reserve one of her favorite scents for Monday mornings, when she wants to get a jumpstart on the week.

- **Teach her to pat dry:** This kind of drying requires more patience, and that's exactly the point. There are times in the day when we need to take an extra minute or two to slow down and give ourselves some loving pats.

- **Teach her to be grateful for her body:** Teach her to acknowledge various body parts when she is rubbing lotion on her skin. She may say, for instance, "My hands helped me whack that ball today" or "My neck has been doing a great job connecting my head to my shoulders."

- **Soften soles:** After a bath, she can smooth lotion on her feet, cover them with plastic bags, pull on socks, and listen to a bedtime story while her feet become silky smooth.

Back to Basics

Fundamentals for Keeping Her at Her Best

As we continue to stretch beyond what we were taught, and as we open ourselves to new possibilities and new ways of seeing life, we must also remember the basics. After all, things are often called basic because they are so essential that we don't think about them anymore. We take them for granted. Yet they are the foundation for the building of body esteem.

(80) Exercise Together

From speed walking to Jazzercise to skipping to weight training to mountain biking to surfing, whatever the chosen activity, parents can ensure that their daughters develop better relationships with their bodies if they exercise together regularly. This is also a good chance for us to model the importance of exercise. Whether a father-daughter, mother-daughter duo, or the entire family is involved in an aerobic activity, your hearts pump faster and more efficiently as blood circulation increases, nourishing and cleansing your organs. Exercise is good for the brain, too, contributing to mental alertness, which can translate into better academic and on-the-job performance. Additional benefits include increased stamina and weight control. And workouts that raise a sweat can improve moods through the release of endorphins—a natural high—and that means you're more likely to enjoy one another's company.

Rita Finkel, a mother of three, who has two teenage girls, believes that sharing a physical activity with your daughter can enhance the level of respect. Her's is a family that enjoys fencing. For Mrs. Finkel it's recreational, while her daughters engage in competitions. "Because I'm familiar with what's required, I have such respect for what my girls do," Mrs. Finkel said. "The competitions can be grueling. So when I see parents screaming at their kids from the sidelines, I wish they could try fencing for one minute. They would never scream at their girls again. They would understand the level of self-mastery required to continue winning or to maintain composure if they're losing."

Despite the many benefits of exercising regularly, by the time girls reach high school, only two thirds, compared with 80 percent of boys, exercise three or more times a week.[1] Your daughter will be more likely to exercise if she has one of her parents as a partner. And if she learns to enjoy physical activity early in life, she's more likely to continue to exercise when she's an adult. According to the Centers for Disease Control and Prevention, elementary school children should exercise a minimum of thirty to sixty minutes a day.[2] But don't let time constraints stop you. Research also suggests that fifteen minutes of physical exercise, if done often enough, may be just as beneficial as more extensive workouts.[3]

You may find that a great deal of encouragement is required to get your girl up and active. That's what happened with Brenda and her daughter, Carolyn, after their family's move to Manhattan. Carolyn had long enjoyed outdoor activities in their northern California city, but the move east meant spending a lot more time indoors, and fewer opportunities for exercise. Brenda suggested that instead of taking the subway they walk the two miles to Carolyn's new school. Carolyn balked at the idea; she agreed only after Brenda offered to give her the money they would save on the fare.

At first, the two-mile walk seemed impossible. Carolyn needed to let off steam about the move, and sometimes the walked ended abruptly when Carolyn stalked off to the nearest subway stop. On the days when they did make it the entire way on foot, Brenda was physically exhausted. But they persisted, and they kept the hour-long walk going, sometimes through subfreezing weather and despite Carolyn's complaints that her classmates considered her mom "mental" for "making her" walk. Six months into their walking, and with much of Carolyn's anger spent, they had a rhythm to their steps and a familiarity with fixtures on New York City's busy streets.

They kept going throughout the first year in their new city and continued into the next. Today they are closer than ever. Did exercising together do it for them? Who can say? What the mother and daughter do know is that they're a lot fitter than they would have been had they been commuting by subway, and they have had the time together they needed to work through a difficult period in their lives.

(81) Help Her to Understand the Importance of a Good Night's Sleep

A poll conducted by the National Sleep Foundation found that, on average, teenagers are getting about two hours less sleep a night than they need. This is unfortunate because a good night's sleep is essential for replenishing the body's reserves. Three or more weeks of sleep loss can weaken your daughter's immune system and make her more susceptible to colds, flu, and other infectious diseases.[4] And if she is sleep deprived she's more likely not only to be irritable and unable to concentrate in class, but to be too tired to exercise or participate in other activities that are beneficial to her health. If she drives, a sleep deficit can also put her at a higher risk for a deadly car accident.

Many of us who have teenagers may assume that since they are practically adults they can get by on much less sleep. But to be at their best, teenagers need about nine hours and fifteen minutes of sleep each night, and elementary school–age children require about forty-five minutes more.[5] What's a parent to do? We're glad you asked. Here are some suggestions:

- **Schedule bedtime:** Even older teenagers may need to have their parents insist that they get enough sleep. Work with your daughter to help make this a priority in her life.

- **Encourage her to catnap:** Explain that many successful professionals have learned to replenish their energy during the day by taking short naps. She may do the same thing during her commute to school or by finding a quiet spot immediately after lunch and before the class bell rings.

- **Be a sleep model:** Schedule enough time to get the sleep you need, so you can model healthy habits for your daughter.

- **End your dependence on coffee:** Don't tell your daughter that you can't function until you've had your cup of coffee. You could be giving her the message that it's OK to use drugs to compensate for her body's natural need for sleep.

- **Change the rules:** Establish and enforce a rule that requires her to complete her homework before she logs on to the Internet, turns on the television, or gets on the phone.

- **Insist on early work schedules:** Support her in refusing jobs or work schedules that require late hours.

(82) Lighten Her Physical Load

Although most of us realize that the bulging backpacks many children tote back and forth to school are harming their backs, few of us do more than give the problem lip service. But by working with your girl to alleviate the problem, you will be helping her to avoid long-term back problems and teaching her to honor her body's main support system. Unfortunately, that's not what's happening with most youngsters. A study by the American Academy of Orthopedic Surgeons reports that 58 percent of orthopedists reported working with children who complain of back and shoulder pain caused by heavy backpacks.[6] Back troubles can damage a child's relationship with her body.

Connie, age fourteen and a freshman at a private school in Connecticut, ignored her mother's entreaties to carry some of her books in her hands so she could lighten her backpack. In the seventh grade, Connie carried a backpack that weighed twenty-five pounds, more than a fourth of what she weighed. By the eighth grade she was suffering with back problems and spent ten months working with a physical therapist. That wasn't the only complication. Once extremely athletic, Connie's injury meant that she had to miss out on her favorite sports. She gained thirty pounds, which only increased the pressure on her back. By the time her health had improved, she was too discouraged to participate in athletic events, and she viewed herself as being too "big and clumsy," as she said, "to play anything that requires me to move my body."

Fortunately, there's much your daughter can do to ensure that her backpack doesn't become a real pain. Our suggestions include making certain that she:

1. **Weighs in:** Once a month, use the family scale to see how much your daughter's backpack weighs. If it's more than 15 percent of her weight, ask her to figure out what she can start leaving behind.

2. **Buys twins:** Work with the parents' association at your daughter's school to raise money for extra sets of textbooks—one for use in the classroom and another to leave at home.

3. **Rolls 'em:** Try to interest your daughter in a backpack on wheels. (Don't force the issue. In many schools they're considered geeky.)

4. **Keeps books close:** The heaviest books should be packed close to the back to prevent an additional burden on the spine.

5. **Buckles up:** Invest in a backpack with a waist strap. A waist strap helps pull weight closer to the body and distribute it more evenly along the hips and pelvic area.

6. **Watches those straps:** Heavy bags slung over just one shoulder make for an uneven distribution of weight, so use both straps. Also, adjust the straps, so the weight sits on the hips, the body's center of gravity.[7]

7. **Bends at the knees:** Explain that while carrying her backpack, if it's necessary to bend over to pick up something, she should bend at the knees rather than just lean forward.

8. **Stands tall:** Cynthia Garmezano, a physical therapist in Manhattan, advises that the better her posture the better your daughter's chances are of having abdominal and trunk control—which will help support her back. (But don't nag her about slouching, either.)

Finally, if you worry that you won't have the time to teach your daughter to mind her back, make an agreement with her. Rather than insist that she clean her room every weekend (or whatever the schedule), let her alternate this chore with back-pack weigh-ins and clean-outs. In the long run you'll be glad you paid more attention to the state of her back than the clutter on her floor.

(83) Teach Her to Care for Her Teeth for a Lifetime

For advice on how to teach our daughters to treat their teeth lovingly, we turned to pediatric dentist Dr. Michael King. Children literally ask to visit him. In Dr. King's activity-filled waiting room on New York's East Side, the videos, jukebox, and a Star Wars human-sized action figure keep his patients smiling. Once they are seated in his miniature dental chair, many children do begin to howl, but with delight. Dr. King, who is also a stand-up comic, appears several times a week at the New York Comedy Club, and he keeps his patients laughing between procedures with one-liners and magic tricks. This Patch Adams of the dental circuit has treated kid celebrities from the stage as well as the screen. He said the best way to teach kids to treat their teeth lovingly is to find them a dentist they love. The following are a list of suggestions that will keep your daughter on the right track for healthy teeth and gums:

- **Practice "preteeth" dental care:** Many parents know it's unhealthy for infants to sleep with bottles because milk held in their mouths causes early decay. The same holds true for nursing babies. Infants shouldn't sleep with a breast nipple in their mouths.

- **Limit fluoride in little mouths:** When you're wiping those first teeth down with a damp, soft cloth and before the first dental visit, limit fluoride toothpaste to just a speck. Too much fluoride can build up in a child's system, eventually causing tooth discoloration.

- **Explain dentists in upbeat terms:** Tell your daughter that the two of you are going to visit someone who will give her a toothbrush, count her teeth, and show her how to brush them. To prevent apprehension, children age nine and under will enjoy the book *Berenstain Bears Visit the Dentist,* by Stan and Jan Berenstain.

- **Find a kid-friendly dentist:** Ask other parents or your daughter's pediatrician for references. The professional you choose should employ strategies that relax children. Techniques may include having the staff dress in nonclinical-looking clothing, giving the child a mirror so she can see what's being done to her teeth, and allowing the parent to remain nearby or to hold the child during the checkup.

- **Schedule the first dental visit after her first year:** The American Academy of Pediatric Dentists recommends scheduling your child's first dental visit around the age of one year, whether or not she has teeth yet.

- **Make the first visit short and sweet:** Even if the dentist discovers a problem, if your daughter is not in pain, postpone the work. "That first visit is the most important," advised Dr. King. "If it takes too long or she gets frightened, you can lose the child."

- **Don't pack fruit snacks in her lunch:** These sticky sweets adhere to teeth and promote decay.

- **Help your child brush:** A lot of children aren't coordinated enough to brush their teeth adequately before they are age nine or ten. If your child resists your help, make a deal with her that allows her to brush in the morning and for you to do it at bedtime. Use a two-minute egg timer or an electric toothbrush with a timer, so she'll know how long to keep brushing.

- **Don't threaten or scold:** In addition to diet and tooth care, dental problems are often heredity. So if she has a cavity, don't make her feel worse than she already does about having one.

- **Clean around braces:** If your daughter has braces or retainers, remember that it's harder to brush adequately, so ask your dentist about using a WaterPik™. These water-flow devices can help remove trapped bits of food from between teeth.

- **Make flossing fun:** Children often hate flossing, so let your daughter listen to a radio or CD player when she flosses, and she'll think of it as something that's fun to do.

(84) Hang Up a Health Bulletin Board

We live in the health-information age. Every week or so, a newspaper story reports the results of a medical breakthrough or study about new, helpful health practices. Magazines, too, have begun to devote sections to health and fitness. It may sometimes seem like information overload, but an abundance of health information is a blessing, not a problem. Fortunately, there is a way to incorporate relevant advice into our lives.

That's why it's important to put up a cork bulletin board solely for health articles and tips. It's a simple step that can send a message to your daughter that good health is a terrible thing to waste. Soon enough, she'll be scanning the news pages for articles to pin up herself.

(85) Teach Her About the Potential for Infection Associated with Popular Trends

General issues of self-care, including how to avoid infections, can be a problem if your daughter isn't paying attention to the basics. Sometimes even the most sensible girls seem to get caught up in popular trends—such as getting tattoos or having their noses, tongues, or navels pierced. These practices can lead to infection, since operators are often ignorant about sterilization techniques.

New York Times health writer Jane Brody has reported that bacteria and viruses can be introduced into the bloodstream during body piercing, causing hepatitis and even transmitting the HIV virus that causes AIDS. There's also the possibility of long-term scarring and initial pain and weeks of soreness while the body recuperates from piercing. Also, tongue piercing can cause soreness, infections, or allergic reactions that can temporarily make speaking difficult or even cause permanent numbness.[8]

Since dire warnings about health hazards seldom discourage adolescents from following popular trends, consider an ongoing series of chats from the perspective of women risking their health and welfare. A perfect time to launch this conversation is during a "nail polish party." Suitable for girls eight years old and up, nail parties can involve just the two of you or a group of her friends, invited to try out new nail polish shades and give each other pedicures and manicures.

Feet are the perfect way to get started on the subject of tattooing or piercing because girls almost always grimace when you tell them about the infections that were caused by the ancient Chinese custom of foot binding. Explain that some time around the eleventh century, foot binding became popular in China. A wife with bound feet signaled that her husband was wealthy, supposedly because he could afford to keep a woman who could not perform heavy labor. Foot binding was a painful and disfiguring practice, and untold numbers of girls ages five and six were forced to submit to having strips of cloth tightly wound around their feet, (so that their toes were pressed into the soles of their feet,) to retard growth. Despite regular bathing and rebinding, bound feet became infected and swollen. Girls who loosened their bandages were shamed, and some were beaten. Their feet eventually became permanently disfigured, and the stench of her own rotting flesh was difficult for the girl to bear. Still, if she grew into a woman with tiny feet, she was showered with compliments and was able to improve her family's future by attracting a wealthy husband.

The practice was outlawed more than ninety years ago, but its telling will deeply shock the nail-party participants. They may groan and waddle on their heels, trying to imagine the restrictions of life with bound feet. As the furor dies down, ask whether they think women still threaten their health and endure pain for the sake of what's in style. This is the perfect time to discuss the hazards of various trends. Ask your daughter what she thinks it means for a girl to risk being silenced for the sake of tongue piercing.

Through the months, as you and your daughter continue this conversation, point out other fashion trends that can endanger a woman's health. You may mention the risk and discomfort associated with shoe styles, such as monster wedgies. These shoes have caused many girls to fall, spraining their arms and ankles. As with bound feet, high wedgies (and high heels, for that matter) make walking and certainly running difficult. Talk also about rumors that some models and Hollywood starlets have had ribs removed so they can retain hourglass shapes. Draw her into a conversation about what it means, both as a symbol and as a matter of health, that women give up ribs for someone else's conception of beauty. By giving your daughter something to think about, rather than one more lecture, you may ensure that she is more likely to make healthy decisions concerning her body.

(86) Become a Water Vigilante

Even adults who are generally good role models for healthy lifestyles forget the eight-glasses-of-water-a-day requirement. Life is so busy and hectic that it seems enough to encourage children to drink milk and fruit juices. However, water is absolutely essential in treating our bodies lovingly. After all, water makes up more than half our body weight. It stands to reason that since we excrete it, we have to restock.

It's important to teach our girls that they shouldn't wait until they're thirsty to drink a glass of water, because by then they're already dehydrated. They may not realize that headaches, constipation, and midday exhaustion may be connected to not drinking enough water. Drinking water also helps sustain one's normal body weight. First, when we confuse thirst for hunger—and this is quite common—we consume unnecessary calories. Second, the regular generous consumption of water actually helps the body burn calories efficiently.[9] Here are suggestions for getting your girl to down the wet stuff:

- **Be a good role model:** Drink plenty of water each day, so you can model for your daughter how to treat her body lovingly.

- **Play the sponge game:** If you have a young child, have her stand at a sink and feel a dry sponge, then ask her to run water over it. Point out that it feels better when it is given water, just like our bodies.

- **Make water pops:** Buy a six pack of twelve-ounce bottled water, pour a few inches from the top of each, pop in a straw to add a festive air, and freeze. In the morning before your daughter heads off for school, wrap a paper towel around a bottle and stick it in her backpack so she can drink it later. (Health purists recommend drinking water that's room temperature, but maybe these folks don't have kids.)

- **Recycle water bottles:** Don't feel you have to keep buying new bottles of water. Wash used bottles and refill them with filtered water.

- **H_2O each morning:** Encourage your daughter to start each morning (before breakfast) with a glass of water.

- **Serve the wet stuff with dinner:** Rather than soft drinks with dinner, place glasses of water beside each dinner plate. Your children will likely drink it because it's within reach.

- **Take water on outings:** Carry frozen bottles of water along with you on family outings, and they'll be a hit.

- **Encourage her to drink water before treats:** Establish a family rule that everyone drinks a glass of water before any treats, such as desserts or sweet snacks.

- **Keep water up front:** A pitcher of filtered water should be the first thing that catches the eye when the refrigerator door is opened, so your daughter will grab it when she's thirsty.

After only a few months of this water barrage, there's a good chance that your daughter will start drinking water without you prompting her to do so.

She Is What She Eats

Feeding the Body Right

Teaching your daughter to eat healthy food is analogous to erecting the foundation of a skyscraper. Healthy foods are the building blocks of the body beautiful.

(87) Create an Environment That Supports Healthy Eating

We made a list of six common food behaviors that can lead your daughter down the road toward a lifetime of healthy eating. If this isn't standard behavior for you, work with your family to transform your habits.

1. **Clear your shelves of junk foods:** A lot of parents reason that it's not fair to siblings who don't have "weight problems" to refuse to restock high-fat, high-sugar snacks and processed foods. But since these foods aren't good for anybody, no one is being deprived by not having them. Instead, buy healthy snacks, such as pretzels and baked corn chips. And always discourage eating "from the bag" and in front of a television set, so your daughter can keep an eye on how much she's consuming.

2. **Serve take-out foods sparingly:** Even if it means doing some advance work on the weekends (preparing casseroles, for instance, or roasting a turkey), reserve take-out foods—which tend to be higher in fat, sugar, and salt—for special occasions. If you do get fast food (and unfortunately, according to one estimate, the typical American consumes approximately three hamburgers and four orders of fries every week)[1], portions should be shared. Whoppers, for instance, are definitely big enough for two people—just ask your server to cut them in half.

3. **Never bribe her with food:** Food bribes are helpful only for animal trainers who want their pets to perform. Most of us realize that we shouldn't bribe or punish

kids with food, but do so anyway. If you return home late from the office or after a long business trip, don't "reward" her for her patience with a pizza. If she hasn't eaten, the two of you can prepare a quick, nutritious meal, and then take a walk together. What could be more rewarding?

4. **Eschew fad diets:** In one of the first studies on eating habits of elementary school children, out of 3,175 students in grades five to eight, 42 percent had dieted, 4.8 percent had induced vomiting, and 2.4 percent had taken diet pills. Three percent had used either laxatives or diuretics to lose weight.[2] Children don't dream up weight-loss measures. They've been watching the adults around them try one fad diet after the next. But they need to hear the truth from us about fad diets: even if they do enable dieters to lose weight, dieters tend to gain it back, plus a little extra. Explain that the most effective and lasting approach for maintaining a healthy weight is eating nutritious, balanced meals—and this includes keeping an eye on caloric intake and engaging in an active lifestyle. You can point out that once an individual starts dieting, she can throw off her metabolism.

5. **Push fruits and vegetables:** Sit down with your children and brainstorm with them about how to get them to include five fruits and vegetables in their diets each day. Your daughter can have juice and a banana with her breakfast, lettuce on a lunch sandwich, an apple or carrots for an after-school snack, and a plate of orange wedges and a vegetable at dinner. It may sound like a lot, but look at it this way: she won't have room to fill up with an excessive amount of non-nutritious food. You may want to pick up a copy of *Eating Well for Optimum Health: The Essential Guide to Food, Diet, and Nutrition,* by Andrew Weil, M.D.

6. **Teach her about calories:** Many of us learned to ignore caloric content when we jumped on the fad diet bandwagon. But most experts now agree that if we want to maintain a healthy weight, we should keep an eye on how many calories we're taking in daily. Rather than encouraging her to be obsessive about every calorie, you can teach her that a general awareness of what she's eating can only add up to a healthy weight.

(88) Prepare Her for Adulthood by Teaching Her How to Prepare Healthy Meals

The idea of teaching daughters to cook isn't as popular as it used to be. Some mothers are hesitant because they believe that if their daughters don't know how to cook, they will be liberated from traditional female roles. Besides, who has the time to teach them, anyway? But your daughter's body is at issue here. Not knowing how to cook may translate into an adult life of processed, packaged, or take-out meals, with an overload of salt, sugar, and fats. And learning to feed oneself lovingly is an important part of self-nurturing. Teaching your daughter to cook will not only help her maintain a healthy weight and body, but it can be lots of fun, too.

The parent, grandparent, godparent, or older sibling who supervises the lesson should not necessarily be the one who is the best cook or the one who usually cooks. In fact, this is a great way to give a parent an evening off from kitchen duty. The meticulous instructions in most cookbooks make it easy to prepare recipes that turn out right the first time, and if your daughter's early efforts are successful, she'll feel encouraged to try again. Besides, when cookbooks are filled with scrumptious-looking photos, they can give novice cooks ideas about presentation.

If your daughter's cooking lessons are the start of a project that is supervised by a favorite adult, that person may enjoy a subscription to *Cooking Light*, a beautifully illustrated magazine.

One of the most important roles for the adult in this activity is to steer your girl's choices toward healthy and nutritious recipes.

Although the adult and child may begin these cooking lessons by focusing on the preparation of one dish, as time goes by it's important to plan subsequent lessons around accompanying dishes, so that eventually your daughter can cook a complete meal. When your daughter finally pulls off this feat independently, she will be filled with satisfaction.

Her sense of accomplishment will grow as she hears the delighted groans and compliments from her parents and siblings. After she has mastered a complete meal, ask her if she's willing to prepare the same meal for newlyweds, an elderly couple, or a needy family. You can contact a local house of worship or other organization that can put you in touch with an appropriate family. When she wraps the still-warm meal, packs it in a basket with disposable tableware, and then delivers it to a grateful household, she will view her new cooking skills with a deep sense of pleasure.

(89) Change Her Notion of Comfort Foods

Depending upon our ethnic backgrounds or unique childhood experiences, many of us remember particular foods with fondness. In our imaginations at least, many of these foods were served by mothers who were devoted to ensuring our every indulgence. No wonder we associate them with "comfort." But though the child inside us wants to eat these rich foods, the calculating adult knows the cost of taking in calories that the body can't use.

Now that we're parents ourselves, we can rewrite the script for our daughters so they can learn to comfort their minds and feed their bodies nourishing foods at the same time. After all, the only real requirement for comfort food is that it should be something that our daughters associate with being cared for.

We can teach our girls to reach for what's healthy by creating warm memories connected to nutritious foods. The next time your daughter is studying, prepare a pot of unsweetened herbal tea for both of you. Present it on a tray with lovely china cups or favorite mugs and cloth napkins. If you sit quietly beside her, perhaps reading, resting, or catching up on your own paperwork, your presence will help her feel nurtured. She may initially complain that the tea is not sweetened, but encourage her to take a few sips. Even if she insists on honey in her tea, remember that it's a lot healthier than a soft drink. And a pot of tea is something you can quickly but lovingly prepare for her. If it's a hot day, one of the new vitamin drinks over ice can be a tasty and refreshing alternative.

If your daughter likes to munch while studying, try the boiled and salted soy beans called "edamame" that are available in many produce marts. Warmed in the microwave or served room temperature, they are not only tasty but, like worry beads, give her something to do with her hands—and distract her from her concerns—as she opens the pods to get to the beans. Other healthy snacks include unbuttered popcorn, thin pretzel sticks, rice cakes, and baby carrots, cherry tomatoes, or red pepper rings with a dollop of low-fat Ranch dressing. On hot days, serve ice pops made from fruit juices.

Another approach to creating indelible memories around foods involves making a big deal out of taking a trip to a produce stand or farmers' market. Children love to spend time on these green outings—looking at various types of tomatoes and beautifully arranged fruits and vegetables. Treat the trip with the same reverence you would reserve for a museum outing, and your daughter will long connect fruits and vegetables with some of her favorite memories.

And don't forget the joy of gardening. Youngsters are more likely to eat vegetables that they have had some experience growing. If you have a backyard, ask your daughter and an adult who is close to her to plant a Mother's Day vegetable garden for you. If space is a concern, create together a Mother's Day window box of herbs, such as basil, or consider a balcony planter of cherry tomatoes.

In the long run, it may be easier to let your daughter associate fried chicken or rice pudding with the term *comfort food* than to prepare something healthy with an extra dose of attention. But the time you invest in healthy food now will make a difference in your daughter's relationship with her body.

(90) Teach Her to Be Discerning About Sugars

Don't give up on the battle of sweets. Many parents apparently have. Although physicians recommend that only 10 percent of our calories should come from added sugar, children in the United States eat about twice that amount. And according to a federal survey, the average girl eats about twenty-four teaspoons of added sugar a day.[3] But that's just *added* sugar. Per capita intake of all sugars has risen by 28 percent in fifteen years, fifty three teaspoons a day by 1997. The difference in calories between the lowest and highest consumers of added sugar is 190 calories a day, which, over the course of a year, points out health writer Jane Brody, can add up to a weight difference of twenty pounds.[4]

Maybe you've already tried getting your girl to cut back on sweets by eliminating sweet sodas, and you just don't have the time to police everything she eats. That's why it's wonderful that you're teaching your daughter to care for her own body. Instead of policing, you can help her choose the right foods by explaining how to identify foods that contain sugars. Once she understands that you are not trying to get her to cut out sugar entirely but simply to curb her consumption, she will be more likely to make the right choices.

First, though, there's probably information you should bone up on. For instance, as Brody points out, the body processes all sugars equally. It doesn't distinguish between the sugar in an orange or the sugar in a candy bar. The significant difference is that the candy offers nothing but sugar, while the orange is filled with essential nutrients. When we fill up with "useless" sugars, we ingest less of the nutritional foods our bodies need.

One of the best starts for broadening your daughter's understanding of sweets is to take her with you on a special "sugar" shopping trip to a supermarket. (Later you can teach her about fats in a similar manner.) Explain that you want to teach her how to make informed choices because too much sugar can contribute to tooth decay and obesity. As you shop together, ask her to help you pick out foods that are good for you and that are low in added sugar. She's probably already aware of the facts concerning candies, puddings, ice creams, and cakes. But as she reaches for items that have high added-sugar contents, such as yogurt, fruit snacks, sweet cereals, sweetened drinks, muffins, and breakfast cereals, you can begin to offer information that she can use for a lifetime. During your "sugar tour," be sure to devote extra attention to items in the soft drink aisle, which includes sodas, fruit punches, lemonades, and drink mixes. If your daughter is old enough to understand figures, explain that there is so much sugar in most soft drinks that drinking an extra one each day can increase an individual's chances of being obese by 60 percent. One researcher suggested that the soft drink's impact on the body may be attributable to the body having trouble adapting to such intense concentrations of sugar taken in liquid form.[5]

Once she has finished her sugar tour, invite her to pick out a treat for herself. You may find that she chooses something that is particularly healthy for her. Even if she doesn't, you'll know that the information you've imparted isn't going to go to waste. She'll be carrying it around in her head on subsequent trips, long after she begins shopping on her own.

(91) If She Becomes a Vegetarian, Support Her Choice

Susan was furious when her sixteen-year-old daughter returned from boarding school last summer and announced that she'd become a vegetarian. Susan said, "She acted like it was a religion and criticized everything we ate. Sometimes she wouldn't sit at the table with us because she said she couldn't stand watching us 'devour flesh.' " As the weeks wore on, Susan's daughter refused anything she labeled "animal products," including eggs, yogurt, milk, meat, poultry, and fish. Worried that her daughter would become undernourished, Susan insisted that she "improve" her diet.

Susan's daughter is not alone in her new approach to eating. According to one poll, 37 percent of the 12.4 million adults who described themselves as vegetarians had children under age eighteen, and 24 percent of those who were vegetarians had at least one child living at home who was also a vegetarian.[6]

In addition to being considered cool, vegetarianism can be a healthy alternative. The American Dietetic Association suggested that when vegetarian diets are "appropriately planned," they can provide adequate nutrition and offer health benefits.[7] Going meatless can mean a diet free of chemical additives, pesticides, and contaminants and reducing the chance of heart disease and cancers.

If you're not a vegetarian and your daughter is, you, like Susan, may be confused by what, for some adherents, seems to be an almost religious devotion to this lifestyle. In fact, some aspects of vegetarianism do have a spiritual dimension. Adherents often see themselves, and all living things, as part of the divine manifestation. Wanting to be "at one" with the universe, they refuse to support the killing of animals.

In the early stages, new vegetarians, especially young ones who like the idea of establishing an identity that's somewhat different from the family, may act like religious fanatics, preaching the gospel of healthy eating whenever the mood strikes. Though these sermons may be annoying and their new dietary requirements initially disruptive, we urge you to develop an appreciation for your daughter's commitment. Try to be grateful that she has chosen a path that, to her, expresses good health and peaceful coexistence.

You and her dad can support your vegetarian daughter by planning nutritious menus with her and becoming familiar with the health benefits, as well as the ethical and environmental concerns, of vegetarians. But there are few hard-and-fast rules about what this eating style includes. It can be helpful to understand the different kinds of vegetarians:

Basic vegetarians avoid meat and consume foods from plant sources.

Vegans avoid all animal products, including honey.

Lacto-ovo vegetarians avoid meat, including poultry and fish, but eat eggs and milk.

Lacto vegetarians avoid eggs, meat, fish, poultry, and seafood, but eat dairy products.

Pesco vegetarians eat fish but no meat.[8]

Pollo vegetarians avoid meat but eat chicken.[9]

Although it's true that vegetarian adolescents must be savvy about getting enough nutrients required for proper growth, they can certainly do so. Writing for the *New York Times,* correspondent Mindy Sink explains that the health concerns about these diets include not getting sufficient protein, vitamins B12 and D, iron, calcium, and zinc (all of which are found in animal sources). Sink writes, "Children need all of those elements for energy, cognitive thought and achieving maximum growth potential with proper tissue and bone density."[10]

Fortunately, there are numerous books that can help you and your daughter learn how to find these nutrients in plant sources. Three books include *A Teen's Guide to Going Vegetarian* and *The Teen's Vegetarian Cookbook,* both by Judy Krizmanic, *and Vegetables Rock! A Complete Guide for Teenage Vegetarians,* by Stephanie Pierson. For more information on vegetarianism from a teenage perspective, subscribe to *How on Earth!*, P.O. Box 3347, West Chester, PA, 19381.

When your daughter is new to vegetarianism, you can teach her how to coexist peacefully with her own family. If necessary, you may want to suggest to your daughter that she earn money to contribute toward purchasing the specialized foods she requires. And as for any fervent messages she may deliver on the dangers of meat, and if she gets overbearing, let her know how it makes you feel. You may say, for instance, "I know you don't feel good about the way I eat. I don't necessarily approve of everything you do, either. But loving and accepting someone and not judging them is part of being in a family. So please don't make me feel judged." The two of you may never see eye to eye on what's served at the table, but that certainly doesn't preclude you from remaining heart to heart.

XII

Safety Issues
Keeping Her Body from Harm

Our daughters deserve to be safe, but the ugly truth is that they are often put in harm's way because they have female bodies. In some regard at least, it would be great if we could cover them with invisible shields that could protect them from anyone who would do them harm. But even if we could, that wouldn't give them the inner strength they need to move about the world with a sense of peace. That's why we must work hard at giving them defense strategies—in the event that they ever need them.

(92) Don't Hit Her

Parents who hit their children don't usually describe it as abuse. They may call it spanking or slapping or paddling because, like their parents—and most child beaters were raised by parents who beat them—they have learned to lie about why they do it. Some prefer the timeworn motto "Spare the rod and spoil the child," despite the fact that all reliable research indicates that using a rod (or hands or anything else) against a child is the actual key to "spoiling." Battered girls, for instance, are much more likely to grow into women who will form relationships marked by physical abuse. Parents also say they beat their children out of love, but love has nothing to do with it.

Parents who spank children do so out of anger—whether contained or overflowing. Their anger is usually connected to past injustices, not simply to a child's misbehavior. The parent strikes out because he or she can get away with it. If you hit your daughter, truthfully consider the most recent event and allow yourself to imagine what she experienced at the hands of someone who is supposed to care for and protect her. If hitting has been a problem for you, you're obviously ready to create change—for you and for your daughter.

The first step to ending this cycle is to acknowledge that you've done something wrong and then promise yourself and your daughter that it will not happen again. Don't try to justify what you've done in the past or blame the child: "It's just that you get me so angry when you . . ." Instead, apologize for your behavior.

If you have a spouse who will not listen to reason and insists on beating your child, do whatever is necessary to ensure your daughter's safety. It may mean consulting a therapist before the next battle, taking your daughter to a shelter, calling 911 and summoning the police, or physically shielding her from harm.

If you're worried that you will lose your temper and hit your daughter again, consider trying one of a number of techniques. Practice counting to ten; in the middle of a confrontation, focus on your feet and force them to walk away; grab a phone and call a child abuse hotline; don't drink, since you're more likely to hit when you feel uninhibited; or enroll in an anger-management class. If you backslide, apologize and explain how difficult it is to break bad habits.

Also spend time writing letters (that you may decide to send) if you had a parent or caregiver who abused you. Tell this person how being hit made you feel and how it is affecting your daughter. Don't downplay what your parents may have done to you. If you were hit, that was abuse, no matter what they may have called it in their culture. The aim is to release some of your rage over your treatment, so you won't do to your daughter what was done to you. You should also consider "pillow" exercises, in which you use a rolled-up towel to beat a pillow that is a stand-in for the parent who hit you. Say out loud how angry you feel about your mistreatment. (Your daughter can also benefit from this rage-release exercise.) After a period of letter writing and pillow therapy, work on forgiving those who have hurt you and forgiving yourself for having hurt your daughter. Holding on to anger and resentment about the beatings you endured is self-defeating and can lead only to more pain for your child.

(93) Teach Her How to Spot a Potentially Dangerous Boy

Ask any girl or woman who has been physically or sexually attacked by someone she knows, and chances are she will tell you that the anger and violence didn't simply come out of the blue. There's a good chance that there were warning signs that she ignored. Your daughter can avoid some threatening situations if you teach her about the warning signs of a potentially abusive mate. Be aware that violent men and boys come from every socioeconomic level, every race and religion. Sometimes parents miss warning signs in a potential abuser because they are blinded by the trappings of his family's financial success.

Since your daughter is more likely to listen to a story than a lecture, the two of you can read together the story that follows. Just before you begin, ask your daughter to be on the lookout for any characteristics that may be considered warning signs of violent boys.

Terry was a girl who was full of spirit and intelligence, and she was so happy when she met a young man who seemed just perfect for her. The boys she'd known before liked to play hard to get. But a few days after she met James, he told her he loved her and begged her to promise she wouldn't date anyone else. Terry was happy to agree and pointed out to her friends that James was not only handsome, but old-fashioned in a cute way. He believed that men should be breadwinners, while women should care for the home and children.

As the weeks progressed, Terry couldn't believe that she hadn't known James most of her life. She was seeing less of her friends, of course, because James wanted all her time and hated sharing her with anyone else. He loved her so much, he even seemed jealous of her family. Poor guy, he must have had his heart broken in the past. Sometimes he seemed to be checking up on her, making sure she was where she said she would be. Their relationship was really intense, and she knew other girls envied her. Terry had even noticed a flash of jealousy in the eyes of Frannie, her best friend since kindergarten. Frannie had walked up when Terry and James were on the lawn in the park across from their school. As usual, she and James had been wrestling together. It was sexy the way he liked to pin down her arms and kiss her.

As Frannie approached them, James whispered that Frannie looked like a "cow." Terry didn't like that kind of talk, but she knew that deep down in his heart James was a hurt little boy who tried to cover up his softness with a tough exterior. Most people fell for his angry act and were a little bit afraid of him. But he really had two personalities: a gruff side he showed to the world and the soft sweetness he reserved for her. He could be hurt so easily, and he complained that no one but she really understood him. He'd confided in Terry about his terrible childhood and how he'd grown up seeing his father beat his mom. He'd joked to Terry that now that he'd told her all his secrets, if she ever left him, he'd have to shoot himself. That scared her a little, but then he started tickling her again and held her down.

When your daughter has finished reading, discuss whether she has been able to spot the eight classic behavioral patterns of abusers that were woven into James's story. Go through the following checklist and discuss how the items played themselves out in James's behaviors.

- **Rushes to love:** Potential abusers view women and girls as property that they must quickly claim, like a coveted item at an auction.

- **Believes in traditional sex roles:** Potential abusers are often male chauvinists, believing that to be attractive, women and girls should be servile and unassertive.

- **Is extremely possessive:** While girls often interpret jealousy as a sign of true love, jealousy can actually reflect a boy's belief that he owns his girlfriend.

- **Is rage-filled:** With a quick-trigger temper and a tendency to ridicule others, particularly women and girls, he is seething with rage and about to explode.

- **Is narcissistic:** His view of himself as a victim of circumstances feeds his secret belief that he has been so badly hurt that he can be concerned only with his own feelings, since no one else will care about him.

- **Enjoys physical domination:** Controlling her with his strength turns him on, even in a wrestling game.

- **Has a history of violence:** His model for how to treat others was shaped in a home in which people were abused.

- **Makes suicide/death threats:** The hidden threat is that if she leaves him, he will kill himself and take her with him.

It's important to familiarize your daughter with these warning signs before she falls head over heels in love. Otherwise she may be blind to warning signs and feel that you are just picking on her boyfriend. As most parents realize, the more you try to discourage a teenager from loving someone, the more likely it is that she will become all the more passionate about being with him.

(94) Teach Her What to Do in the Event of an Assault

We pray that our daughters will never be assaulted, but it is our responsibility as parents to teach them how to defend themselves. Although discussing these strategies with your daughter will be helpful, it can be much more helpful for the two of you to act out the scenarios, so she can brainstorm with you about how to handle difficult situations.

- **Get centered:** Use your experience of being calm under pressure to consider whether it's safe to resist.

- **Tap into your anger:** Don't worry about being nice or sweet. Roar like a wild animal and shout no and (if he's unarmed) put up the fight of your life, kicking, punching, and jabbing.

- **Don't use euphemisms:** Avoid vague terms, such as "Don't touch me down there" or "What you're doing is wrong." Call it for what it is. Say "Stop! This is rape!"

- **Use the power of your eyes:** Turn your eyes into search-lights, seeking every possible means of escape or to summon help.

- **Lie:** Try to convince him that someone will be coming along any minute or that you have a sexually transmitted disease or that you're having an asthma attack or that you are about to vomit.

- **Act crazy:** Pretend you have lost your mind and have a personality disorder that switches from one personality to the next; also talk to the walls and unseen "others."

- **Resist transport:** If he's willing to hurt you where you are, he's sure to do even worse when he gets you someplace where he feels safer. So do everything you can to remain in a place where someone else may come across you or hear your screams.

- **Choose life:** Don't get killed rather than submit. If he is holding a gun to your head or a knife to your throat, for instance, it is better that you give in and save your life.

(95) Teach Her How to Avoid Dangerous Situations

Ask your daughter to imagine a character in a video game whom she's trying to steer through a safe course. Ask her to fill in the blanks by asking herself, "What does Zena need to do to remain safe?"

> *When we first see Zena, she's saying good-bye to her friends just inside the entrance to a club where they've had an evening of fun and laughter. Before Zena takes off she (1)_____, then reapplies her lipstick, while making sure that she has remembered to include a (2)_____. Just before she steps outside, she's joined by Tony, a cute guy she met earlier, so she (3)_____. Once outside, Tony asks if she is thirsty and offers her a sip of the soda he's carrying.*

Zena decides to (4)_____. She doesn't like the idea of being alone on a dark street with a stranger, but she doesn't want to hurt his feelings, so she (5)_____. He understands that she wants to take off and asks for her phone number. She (6)_____. Now that it's late, Zena thinks the best way to get home is in a cab. But first she needs money and remembers that there's an instant teller machine right down the street. She knows (7)_____ and decides it would probably be a better idea to (8)_____. Zena figures that she's looking good because even before she can leave the front of the club, some other guys start flirting with her. Zena's response is to (9)_____. She calls a cab from (10)_____, but before she gets in, she (11)_____.

It turns out she does get together with Tony. He invites her over for a home-cooked meal, but she (12)_____.

Now check the answers your daughter filled in against those we've listed below, and then go through the scenario again and see if your daughter has improved her chances of getting Zena home safely. Be sure to discuss with your daughter why these strategies are safe bets.

1. phones someone in advance to signal she's on her way home.

2. whistle just in case she needs it when she's by herself.

3. introduces him to the bartender and to her friends.

4. refuse any drinks that she hasn't seen being opened.

5. risks being rude anyway, knowing her safety comes first.

6. asks for his number instead.

7. it's a bad idea to get cash from a machine at night

8. use her emergency money.

9. go back inside the club.

10. the bar,

11. gives the bartender or her friends the name of the cab company she called.

12. has a policy of not going to the homes of men she doesn't know, so she makes plans to meet him at a restaurant. They have a great time together, and Zena is feeling fine because she knows how to look out for herself.

(96) Enroll Her in a Self-Defense Class

Self-defense training can feel empowering because it allows a girl to move through the world with an appropriate sense of caution but without fear. The first time Carol, a thirty-one-year-old nurse, watched her ten-year-old daughter flip a 170-pound man over her back during an Aikido demonstration, she understood what it meant to raise a strong girl.

Whether you live in a city or a midsize town, you'll probably have a variety of self-defense classes to choose from, specializing in kung fu, karate, judo, jujitsu, tae kwon do, aikido, or kick boxing. The discipline your daughter selects depends largely on her personality. Ask your husband, a sister or grandparent, godparent or baby-sitter to accompany her to a few sites before she makes a choice.

YWCA centers, which usually offer martial arts courses, are often an excellent, cheaper alternative to expensive private centers. Or ask an instructor whether she would be willing to discount costs if you organized a group. By posting the formation of a girls' group on a school bulletin board or newsletter, you'll find plenty of other parents who are eager to sign up their daughters and willing to share transportation responsibilities. If your daughter is a teenager and you no longer need to set up rides for her, you may still encourage her to invite a friend to take the class with her.

If she resists the idea of self-defense training, you may want to encourage her by sharing the video, *Crouching Tiger, Hidden Dragon,* in which the fearless female characters execute kung fu kicks and jumps with grace and deftness. You may also want to introduce her to the young adult book series Fearless, by Francine Pascal. Although the language is at times salty (nothing you wouldn't overhear in a girls' locker room), the seventeen-year-old heroine, Gaia, who is trained in kung fu, karate, judo, jujitsu, and kickboxing, gives readers an idea of what it means to be unafraid of the world. Gaia is so self-assured, in fact, that after she has eaten doughnuts and wants to work off some of her extra calories, she occasionally roams city parks at night looking for cretins who want to victimize girls, so she can kick their . . . Well, we'll let you and your daughter discover for yourselves. Despite Gaia's Thelma-and-Louise approach to life, if you're lucky, you'll discover that martial arts groups that are heavy on girlpower tend to have a kinder, gentler atmosphere.

(97) Use Role-Playing to Teach Her to Say No to Drugs and Alcohol

Role-playing can be fun for parents and children. The term generally refers to an improvisational acting style in which participants take turns playing characters in a situation. Children enjoy role-playing because it gives them a chance to poke fun at their parents and, at the same time, to convey some of the pressures they face on a day-to-day basis. Parents enjoy role-playing because it gives them a sense of control over their children's lives. When you consider some of the serious problems a child can create by making the wrong decisions, it can be reassuring to know that you and your child have worked out strategies for avoiding trouble.

You will be doing a tremendous service to your girl if you explain to her that it's not just illegal drugs that spell trouble but alcohol, too. People seldom realize just how often alcohol is involved in violent situations. Individuals who may be violence prone, but who are generally able to curb their instincts when sober, often discover that liquor diminishes their reserve. Your role-playing should include situations that not only prepare your daughter to refuse illegal drugs and alcohol, but can get her out of potentially problematic situations.

For all the fun and laughter involved in these minidramas, the most important aspect of role-playing is that there's a good chance that your child, despite peer pressure, can make life-enhancing choices. Young people will tell you that despite warnings from parents, they accepted drugs or alcohol from peers because they were trying to save face. Many feel they may have said no if they'd only known how. This is your chance to work through scenarios that allow your daughter to say no and walk away with her ego intact.

You can introduce role-playing techniques during a family gathering or simply plan time together after a meal. Agree on a situation that you can act out. For instance, you may say, "You're at a party with your girlfriends. Everyone else is trying out marijuana, and now they're trying to convince you that you should use some, too." From there, act out the parts. First, one parent can play your daughter, and your daughter can play one of her friends. Then switch roles. When she has helped you to understand the degree of pressure she sometimes feels, you can try again. If there are more than two people in your family, let the other family member engage in the next scenario. Keep this up for ten to fifteen minutes, working out different scenarios until your daughter hits upon refusals that work for her. Possible answers may include, "No thanks, I'm cool." Or, "Are you kidding? I like my eyes blue, not red." Your daughter is likely to come up with much better responses. Work on these role-playing exercises from time to time. You'll be glad you did.

XIII

Positive Sexuality
Loving All of Who She Is

We just want our daughters to be "good" girls, right? But does good include denying sexual feelings? Perhaps this is what motivates concerns about sex education in the schools. Many parents of children in schools in the United States where sex education is taught refuse to allow teachers to discuss how to prevent pregnancy. Others admit they find it difficult to discuss sex with their children. The price for this silence certainly includes high rates of teenage pregnancy. It's glaringly obvious that no one has to tell young people about their sexuality. According to a Ladies' Home Journal *survey, by the age of thirteen, one of every twelve children is no longer a virgin, and by fifteen, a third of girls and 45 percent of boys have had sex. And half of all teenagers have engaged in oral sex.[1] Denying one's sexuality is a denial of the body itself and, in this way, discourages self-control. That's why it's so important that we teach our daughters to love and respect their sexuality, as well as every other aspect of their bodies.*

(98) Use Books, Television, and
Videos to Enhance Talks About Sex

If one goal for your daughter includes ensuring that she does not think of sex as something "dirty" or as a subject to be avoided, there are a number of books available for children age four and older that can help make this complicated subject easy to talk about. One of the best sex education books available for you to read to a child age four to nine is *What's the Big Secret? Talking about Sex with Girls and Boys,* by Laurie Krasny Brown, an educator, and illustrated by Marc Brown, creator of the "Arthur" books. This book is not only fun and informative, but doesn't shy away from important truths, including the fact that grown-ups engage in sexual intercourse because it feels good.

This is the level of candor you will want to strive for, whatever your convictions may be, if you hope to keep your daughter talking through the years about this important subject. During her adolescence, you may want to schedule times together for sharing a television drama that focuses on teenage life. One show, broadcast at the time of this writing, is *Caitlin's Way,* starring Lindsay Felton, on Nickelodeon. We mention this one in particular because the main character is fully engaged with life.

Although we advise against a steady diet of television, we do think it can be a great learning tool when it leads to a discussion between a parent and child about contemporary issues. Whichever show you share, the hope is that this relaxed time together will give your daughter a chance to open up to you about what she's seeing in her peer group and the pressures she may be feeling.

This may also be a time when your daughter asks you about your sexual history. You certainly shouldn't feel obligated to bare your soul. Your daughter is asking for guidance. But if you have some regrets about your sexual past, try in advance to figure out why.

Many parents who came of age during the "free-love" era and who had many sexual partners now realize there was never anything free about that period. Some marriages and families were destroyed that may have later flourished had the partners been committed to monogamy. And despite all the talk of commitment-free sex, you'd have a hard time finding individuals from that period who went from partner to partner and didn't experience sad times in between. Though they may have felt free to control the physical aspects of sex, they couldn't control any disappointment they may have felt when the affairs ended. This feeling of disappointment is connected to who we are as human beings. When we have orgasms, our bodies release oxytocin, the hormone that is also released during breast-feeding, which promotes strong bonding.

If you do have regrets about your sexual history, you may decide to explain to your daughter that given what you now know about sex, you hope that she will make wiser and more self-loving decisions than you did. You may want to encourage her to wait for marriage or until she's certain that she is in a long-term committed relationship before she chooses to share the gift of her body with someone.

You certainly don't want to do all the talking during these conversations. Your role will be to draw her out, ask her what a certain situation feels like for her, and occasionally offer a few words that reflect your own opinions. When you look back at these times, you'll realize they allowed you subtly to shape the conversations around your belief that in all things, at all times, you want your daughter to behave in a way that honors her body.

(99) Encourage the Teaching of Reproductive Science in Biology Class

As a concerned parent, you can get involved in shaping the curriculum at your daughter's school. In addition to sex education classes—for instruction in how to prevent unwanted pregnancies and sexually transmitted diseases—human reproduction should become part of your daughter's science curriculum. This seems to help children understand the gravity of the subject. Students in grades five and up can begin learning about the miracle of life in discussions that include cell biology, asexual and sexual cell division, and animal reproduction and development, with attention paid to human reproduction, including an overview of the anatomy and physiology of the male and female reproductive systems.

You may want to do some research in your area to locate schools that utilize this approach. If you visit one of these classes, you may see a teacher pointing to a chart of the male and female reproductive systems, and students may show signs of having memorized every detail—from the seminal vesicle (which produces a substance to keep sperm alive) to the uterus. Learning about sex by having to know every detail of how a fertilized egg eventually becomes a baby is education at its best. A course such as this takes the mystery (but not the wonder) out of a subject that can make all the difference in the lives of our daughters.

(100) Don't Be in Denial About the Possibility of Sexual Abuse

Shirley, a thirty-seven-year-old domestic who once struggled to pay the rent, was fully enjoying this day. Her twenty-one-year-old daughter was graduating from an Ivy League college and had been accepted to a leading medical school. The young woman was surrounded by well-wishers, but she rushed toward her mother to thank her for years of support and love. Later, when a reporter from the student paper asked how Shirley had gotten her daughter this far in life, rather than offer a romantic response, she said, "I kept her safe from sexual predators." If Shirley sounds angry, you've got her pegged right. She's furious about parents being in denial about the dangers that exist.

Shirley has learned that for girls to reach womanhood with

their souls intact, their parents must be ferocious in their defense. An estimated one in five girls has been sexually abused. Too many parents of abused girls say, "I didn't know it was happening." That is not an acceptable excuse. We urge you to be aware of the possibility and to protect your daughter. No one protected Shirley.

As a girl, Shirley was an avid reader who hoped to become a scientist. At fourteen, she and her mother left Haiti to live with relatives in Miami. But only months later, everything changed. An older female cousin sexually abused Shirley. She says the abuse occurred for more than two years and practically under her mother's nose, but her mother claims she knew nothing about it. Shirley eventually dropped out of school, ran away from home, and at sixteen became pregnant from a boyfriend. She says today, "The day my daughter was born, I promised her I would never look the other way. There is no excuse. If someone holds a knife up to a child's throat and draws blood, we couldn't just get away with saying 'I didn't see.'"

At the same time, Shirley believes it's important that we do not fill our daughters with fear. "I didn't suspect everyone, but I never ruled out the possibility that something could happen, and when she got older, I taught her that there were a few bad apples out there."

Some will say that Shirley's painful experience drove her to go overboard. The truth is, though, that when it comes to protecting our daughters from sexual abuse, we have to be a little crazy. A lapse in judgment can be dangerous. The following are some suggestions that can help you protect your daughter from sexual predators:

- When checking references for potential child-care workers, talk to parents who have children who are old enough to talk and recall being cared for by this individual.

- Whether contracting with a home-care worker or a preschool, make it a practice of dropping by at unscheduled times so you can check on your daughter. If you are unable to leave work, ask a friend or relative to check for you.

- When your daughter is still young enough for you to over-power her, don't remove her clothes at bed- or bath time, unless you have her permission—even if she's having a tantrum. Instead, if she can't or won't do it herself, ask her if you may remove an article of her clothing or bathe a certain part of her body. (If she refuses, let her sleep in her clothes.) This way, you'll be teaching her that she can control what happens to her body.

- Keep in mind that adolescent girls are frequently targeted for abuse. Role-play with your daughter, teaching her to say loudly and clearly, "I'm not comfortable with this, and I want you to stop."

- If you were a victim of sexual abuse during your childhood, make every effort necessary to heal this area of your life. Parents who have unhealed sexual wounds can unwittingly put their children in harm's way, setting them up to repeat their own childhood scripts.

(101) Show Her How to Fight Sexual Harassment

A boy may grope a girl or make a comment about the size of her breasts. Perhaps he shows her lewd photographs, draw-ings, or graffiti or refers to her in the crudest of terms. Unfor-tunately, this could be occurring anywhere in almost any school. Some boys may view these kinds of hostile acts as teas-ing, but in truth they constitute sexual harassment. A lot of schools have instituted zero-tolerance policies, but respect can't be mandated. And most teachers and administrators are just too busy to notice anything but the most extreme forms of harassment.

"Sometimes the boys can be so wild that when I drive my daughter to school, I feel like I'm dropping her off at the entrance to a jungle," said Grace, the mother of a sixteen-year-old. "One boy grabs his crotch when she walks by and pretends he's having an orgasm."

Grace would like to employ a standard procedure for handling these situations. She has encouraged her daughter to report the inappropriate behavior to a teacher, and if this action doesn't help, she wants to keep upping the ante for the boy. She and her daughter have started keeping track of the dates and details of each incident, as well as the names and phone numbers of witnesses. If warnings don't help, Grace wants to contact the principal, the parents of the offender, or the police if necessary. But Grace feels that her hands are tied. As is the case with so many girls who are sexually harassed, her daughter worries about retaliation. "She told me to just let it go, but she looks miserable. I'd like to wring that little bastard's neck for him."

We hope that your daughter will never be in a similar situation, but if she is, support her if she wants to take action and remind her that she has a right to be educated and that her education shouldn't have to occur in a hostile environment. If possible, though, long before any situation occurs you (and/or her father or siblings) can use role-playing techniques to teach your girl how to communicate her displeasure. Her initial responses may make the difference between whether or not a boy continues to harass her. Explain that she must be unsmiling and unequivocal. She may say something like, "Stop, I don't like that!" Demonstrate how she may feel pressured by onlookers—who seem amused by her harasser's behavior—just to laugh it off.

Also teach your daughter that if the boy bothers her a second time, she can talk to some friends (including some male classmates) to see if they'd be willing to confront him as a group. This way, your girl will feel more comfortable standing her ground and saying, "I've told my friends what you did, and they don't like it either. If you keep it up, we'll confront you in class, on the playground, or wherever." Of course, she should be instructed not to make any threats if her safety is at risk.

Standing up to a potential harasser while being backed up by a group of friends will give your daughter an all-over glow, and you can imagine why. If the confrontation were a scene from a film, there would be a swell of music as the group approaches the bully. The star, in the presence of her allies, would communicate a manifesto: that she has the right to be there in her feminine body and to make her wishes known. And you just know there would be some irrepressible soul watching this film, who would get caught up in the moment and call out, "Aww right! The girls are in the house." And so they are.

IN CONCLUSION

Why Goodness Counts
in the Body

W e have attempted to broaden your understanding of how to raise girls who feel peaceful in their bodies. But we want to remind you that all the self-esteem in the world cannot compensate for moral and spiritual growth in your daughter. Admittedly, morality is a word that has often been misused, like a whip that induces pain and shame. The truth, however, is that morality isn't about how to avoid being bad. It's about discerning the good and developing habits and practices to support it.

Volunteerism, for example, imparts humility and gratitude. A haughty and arrogant woman, despite her good looks, may not seem beautiful to those who spend time with her. At the same time, a child who is taught to be accepting of all people, regardless of racial, ethnic, or religious differences, will grow up feeling that she, too, is acceptable to others. A child taught to appreciate the natural environment moves with confidence, in the understanding that she is part of a larger universe and that she has come into existence through tiny steps over millions of years.

As for your daughter's spiritual growth, whether or not you and your family are members of an organized religion, consider the idea that the Creator is within us as well as around us. If your family does observe a religious tradition, explore ways within that tradition in which you can encourage in your daughter a sense of God's presence within her. There's nothing new about this belief. In Jewish tradition, for example, petitioners ask God to ". . . renew a right spirit within me . . ." (Psalm 51). In the Christian tradition, the apostle Paul asks, "Do you not know that you are God's temple and that God's spirit dwells within you?" (1 Corinthians 3:16). Those words were of course written long ago, but scientific research has since demonstrated the power of the inner spirit. As you may know, studies indicate that when people unite their spirits in prayer, they can create powerful results.

You can easily demonstrate the concept that our bodies are empowered by the spirit within. If your daughter likes to paint, for instance, pick up one of her brushes and explain that her most recent painting is the result of the creative fire of her imagination, not because of the excellent bristles of her brush. If your daughter plays softball, point to her glove and explain that she caught her last fastball because of the energy and strength that she harnessed in her body, not because it's a good glove. Tell her that our bodies have the same relationship to the spirit. Our bodies are the instruments of God; we are empowered by the spirit within.

You can also interject some humor into this subject. If your daughter is thirteen or older, consider renting the video *Down to Earth,* starring Chris Rock. You'll not only find yourself laughing along with this film but afterwards, you can underscore the essential message: although the main character, a well-intentioned would-be comic, changes from one body to another, the young woman continues to love him. It's his spirit that counts.

Whatever means you may use to convey to your daughter the relationship of the body to the spirit, we hope you share our opinion that it is the one key that pulls all of our 101 suggestions together. Just look into the eyes of a girl whose spirit remains intact, and you will feel hopeful about the future. You'll will be reminded that you are in the presence of a young woman who has the power to shape the world according to her vision of good.

The need to live up to the challenge of shaping the world stands before our daughters in ways that were never true before. For example, if forecasts are even partially correct about the potentials from our forthcoming technologies in genetics and computer applications, then humankind is heading into an era when choices will have to be made about how we see ourselves and how we shape our destinies. Resolving these questions won't be a matter of interesting philosophical reflection. The strengths and virtues our daughters bring to these questions will have an enormous impact on the future.

As leaders and mothers of tomorrow, our daughters must learn today how to free themselves from exterior distractions so they can look within themselves for strength and wisdom. Although it's true that the emerging information of the new millennium gives us vast knowledge of this world, our daughters will never lose their need for a moral vision to guide them in the application of the power they will possess. By feeling peaceful in their bodies, they can focus on their individual uniqueness as well as recognize the similarities they have to one another. In this way, they can act in the name of goodness for the life of the world to come.

NOTES

Introduction

1. *The Ad and the Ego*, transcript from the video available from www.newsreel. org/transcri/adandego.htm on February 23, 2001.

2. Shaila K. Dewan, "Central Park Victims Describe Police Inaction on Pleas," *New York Times*, June 13, 2000, available from www.archives.nytimes.com.

3. David Barstow and C. J. Chivers, "A Volatile Mixture Exploded into Rampage in Central Park," *New York Times*, June 17, 2000, A1, B7.

4. Al Baker, "Sex and Power vs. Law and Order," *New York Times*, January 28, 2001, 21.

5. Sara Shandler, *Ophelia Speaks* (New York: HarperCollins, 1999), 4.

6. Leslie Berger, "A New Body Politic: Learning to Like the Way We Look," *New York Times*, July 18, 2000, D7.

7. Martin M. Antony, Ph.D., and Richard P. Swinson, M.D., *When Perfect Isn't Good Enough: Strategies for Coping with Perfectionism* (Oakland, Calif.: New Harbinger, 1998), 230.

8. Berger, "A New Body Politic: Learning to Like the Way We Look."

9. Dan Vergano, "There's Less of Miss America to Love," *USA Today*, March 22, 2000, 6D.

10. Sharon Begley, "What Families Should Do," *Newsweek*, July 3, 2000, available from www.Newsweek.msnbc.com.

11. Vergano, "There's Less of Miss America to Love."

12. Antony and Swinson, *When Perfect Isn't Good Enough: Strategies for Coping with Perfectionism*, 40–41.

13. Sandra Lee Bartky, "Foucault, Femininity, and the Modernization of Patriarchal Power," in *The Politics of Women's Bodies: Sexuality, Appearance and Behavior*, edited by Rose Weitz (New York: Oxford University Press, 1998), 28.

14. Eric Nagourney, "Vital Signs: Passing Along the Diet-and-Binge Habit," *New York Times*, October 3, 2000, F8.

15. Geoffrey Cowley, "Generation XXL," *Newsweek*, July 3, 2000, available from www.Newsweek.msnbc.com.

16. The Associated Press, "Extra Soft Drink Is Cited as Major Factor in Obesity," *New York Times*, February 16, 2001, available from nytimes.com.

CHAPTER ONE

1. George Howe, "The Healing Power of Touch," *Life*, (August 1997): 52.

2. John O'Neil, "Less Pacifier Use, Fewer Ear Infections," *New York Times*, September 12, 2000, F8.

3. Gina Kolata, "While Children Grow Fatter, Experts Search for Solutions," *New York Times*, October 19, 2000, A26.

4. Carolyn Hagan, "Come On Baby, Do the Locomotion," *Child* (September 2000): 36–38.

5. C. Claiborne Ray, "Science Q&A: Stroller Potatoes," *New York Times*, December 5, 2000, available from www.archives.nytimes.com.

6. Miriam Nelson, Ph.D., "Miracle Moves That Save Your Bones," *Prevention* (October 2000): 113.

7. Ibid.

CHAPTER TWO

1. Patricia Anstett, "Mature Girls, a Tangle of Unhealthy Behaviors," *Seattle Times*, February 4, 1998, available from seattletimes.nwsource.com.

2. Julie K. L. Dam, "How Do I Look?" *People* (September 4, 2000): 114–18.

3. Michelle Joy Levine, *I Wish I Were Thin, I Wish I Were Fat* (Huntington Station, N.Y.: Vanderbilt Press, 1997), 141.

4. Michelle Healy, "A Better Life: Food Restriction Linked to Low Self-Esteem," *USA Today*, January 9, 2001, 8D.

5. Levine, *I Wish I Were Thin, I Wish I Were Fat*, 84.

6. Amy Dickinson, "Like Mother, Like Daughter," *Time* (February 5, 2001): 68.

7. Arlie Hochschild with Anne Machung, *The Second Shift* (New York: Avon Books, 1989), 3.

8. Sandra Lee Bartky, "Foucault, Femininity, and the Modernization of Patriarchal Power," in *The Politics of Women's Bodies: Sexuality, Appearance, and Behavior*, edited by Rose Weitz (New York: Oxford University Press, 1998), 30.

CHAPTER THREE

1. Brenda Lane Richardson, "Let There Be Fathers: World Rediscovering Dad, the Nurturer," *Tribune*, June 16, 1985, B5.

2. Kate Zernike, "Girls a Distant Second in Geography Gap Among U.S. Pupils," *New York Times*, May 31, 2000, B5.

3. Virginia Beane Rutter, *Celebrating Girls: Nurturing and Empowering Our Daughters*, (Berkeley, Calif.: Conari Press, 1996), 66.

4. Sandra Lee Bartky, "Foucault, Femininity, and the Modernization of Patriarchal Power," in *The Politics of Women's Bodies: Sexuality, Appearance, and Behavior*, edited by Rose Weitz (New York: Oxford University Press, 1998), 34–35.

5. Leslie Berger, "A New Body Politic: Learning to Like the Way We Look," *New York Times*, July 18, 2000, D7.

6. Judith Kaufman, "Adolescent Females' Perception of Autonomy and Control," in *Females and Autonomy: A Life-span Perspective*, edited by Margot B. Nadine and Florence L. Denmark (Boston: Allyn and Bacon, 1999), 49.

CHAPTER FOUR

1. Michelle Joy Levine, *I Wish I Were Thin, I Wish I Were Fat* (Huntington Station, N.Y.: Vanderbilt Press, 1997), 68.

2. Betsy Cohen, *The Snow White Syndrome* (New York: Macmillan, 1986), 33.

3. Daniel Goleman, *Emotional Intelligence* (New York: Bantam Books, 1995), 100.

4. Anne Jarrell, "The Face of Teenage Sex Grows Younger," *New York Times*, April 2, 2000, Sec. 9, p. 8.

5. Mary Williams Walsh, "Summer Work Is Out of Favor with the Young," *New York Times*, June 18, 2000, A1.

6. Colette Dowling, *The Frailty Myth: Women Approaching Physical Equality* (New York: Random House, 2000), 53.

7. Dowling, *The Frailty Myth: Women Approaching Physical Equality*, xxi.

CHAPTER FIVE

1. Helen Cordes, "Caffeinkids' Parents Ignore Risks of Guzzling 'Power' Drinks," *Portland Press Herald*, May 17, 1998, available from www.NorthernLights.com.

2. Kara Corridan, "Health and Safety Bulletin: News to Protect Your Child" *Child* (September 2000): 30.

3. Jane E. Brody, "Added Sugars Are Taking a Toll on Health," *New York Times*, September 12, 2000, F8.

4. Cordes, "Caffeinkids' Parents Ignore Risks of Guzzling 'Power' Drinks."

5. Brody, "Added Sugars Are Taking a Toll on Health."

6. Cordes, "'Caffeinkids' Parents Ignore Risks of Guzzling 'Power' Drinks."

7. Roberta Smith, "Glossy Portrait of the Artist as a Young Woman," *New York Times,* July 5, 2000, B5.

8. Gina Bellafante, "Body Image Summit," *New York Times,* June 27, 2000, B9.

9. Tamar Lewin, "Children's Computer Use Grows, but Gaps Persist, Study Says," *New York Times,* January 22, 2001, A11.

10. Jane E. Brody, "Fitness Gap Is America's Recipe for Fat Youth," *New York Times,* September 19, 2000, F8.

11. Robert Schwebel, Ph.D., *How to Help Your Kids Choose to Be Tobacco-Free: A Guide for Parents of Children Ages 3 Through 19* (New York: Newmarket Press, 1999), 9.

12. Brad Evenson, "Candy Cigarettes Used to Lure Children to the Real Thing," *National Post,* August 4, 2000, A1.

CHAPTER SIX

1. Michael D. Lemonick, "Teens Before Their Time," *Time* (October 30, 2000): 68.

CHAPTER SEVEN

1. Linda Villarosa, "Evaluating Pains and Gains of Weight Lifting Regimen," *New York Times,* August 29, 2000, F8.

2. Jane E. Brody, "Fitness Gap Is America's Recipe for Fat Youth," *New York Times,* September 19, 2000, F8.

3. Brenda Lane Richardson, *Guess Who's Coming to Dinner: Celebrating Interethnic, Interfaith, and Interracial Relationships* (Berkeley, Calif.: Wildcat Canyon Press, 2000), 6.

4. Natalie Angier, "Who Is Fat? It Depends on Culture," *New York Times,* November 7, 2000, F1.

5. Mashadi Matabane, "Eating Disorders Begin to Plague Black Teens," *New York Amsterdam News,* January 18–24, 2001, 37.

6. Brian Lanker, *I Dream a World: Portraits of Black Women Who Changed America* (New York: Stewart, Tabori & Chang, Inc., 1989), 140.

CHAPTER EIGHT

1. Eric Nagourney, "Vital Signs: Sick in the Head, and in the Stomach," *New York Times,* September 9, 2000, F8.

2. Linda Marsa, "Chest Concerns," *Seventeen* (July 2000): 102.

3. Brenda Lane Richardson and Dr. Brenda Wade, *What Mamma Couldn't Tell Us About Love* (New York: HarperCollins, 1999), 116.

4. Laura Day, *Practical Intuition in Love* (New York: HarperCollins, 1998) 14.

5. Niravi Payne and Brenda Lane Richardson, *The Language of Fertility* (New York: Random House, 1997), 147.

6. Erica Goode, "Women Are Found to Respond to Stress by Social Contact, Not by Fight or Flight," *New York Times*, May 19, 2000, A20.

7. This list was compiled, in part, by Charles Whitfield in *Healing the Child Within* (Deerfield Beach, Fla.: Health Communications, 1987), 84.

8. Michelle Joy Levine, *I Wish I Were Thin, I Wish I Were Fat* (Huntington Station, N.Y.: Vanderbilt Press, 1997), 73.

9. Dan Vergano, "There's Less of Miss America to Love," *USA Today*, March 22, 2000, 6D.

10. Esther Drill, Heather McDonald, and Rebecca Odes, *Deal with It! A Whole New Approach to Your Body, Brain, and Life as a Gurl*, (New York: Pocket Books, 1999), 185–86.

11. Martin M. Antony, Ph.D. and Richard P. Swinson, M.D., *When Perfect Isn't Good Enough: Strategies for Coping with Perfection* (Oakland, Calif.: Harbinger Publications, 1998), 41.

12. "Poor Eating Affects Girl Athletes' Bones," *USA Today*, September 7, 2000, 11D.

13. Martin M. Antony, Ph.D. and Richard P. Swinson, M.D., *When Perfect Isn't Good Enough: Strategies for Coping with Perfection,* 41.

14. Esther Drill, Heather McDonald, and Rebecca Odes, *Deal with It! A Whole New Approach to Your Body, Brain, and Life as a Gurl*, 185–86.

CHAPTER NINE

1. Jennifer Barker Woolger and Roger J. Woolger, *The Goddess Within: A Guide to the Eternal Myths That Shape Women's Lives* (New York: Ballantine Books, 1987), 291.

2. Joan Borysenko, Ph.D., *A Woman's Book of Life: The Biology, Psychology, and Spirituality of the Feminine Life Cycle* (New York: Riverhead Books, 1996), 53.

3. Jane Gross, "In Quest for the Perfect Look, More Girls Choose the Scalpel," *New York Times*, November 29, 1998, available from www.archives.nytimes.com.

4. Susan M. Love, M.D., with Karen Lindsey, *Dr. Susan Love's Breast Book* (Reading, Mass.: Perseus Books, 1990), 25.

5. Eve Ensler, *The Vagina Monologues,* (New York: Villard Books, 1994), 4.

6. Jane E. Brody, "What Could Be Good About Morning Sickness? Plenty," *New York Times*, June 6, 2000, F7.

7. Michael Lewis, "Having Her Say at the See," *New York Times Magazine*, June 4, 2000, 62–64.

8. John P. Conger, Ph.D., *The Body in Recovery: Somatic Psychotherapy and the Self* (Berkeley, Calif.: Frog Ltd., 1994), 62.

9. Christiane Northrup, M.D., *Women's Bodies, Women's Wisdom: Creating Physical and Emotional Health and Healing* (New York: Bantam Books, 1994), 104.

10. Jeanne Elium and Don Elium, *Raising a Daughter* (Berkeley, Calif.: Celestial Arts, 1994), 20.

CHAPTER TEN

1. Patricia Anstett, "Mature Girls, a Tangle of Unhealthy Body Behaviors," *Seattle Times*, February 10, 1998, available from www.Northernlights.com.

2. Jane E. Brody, "Fitness Gap Is America's Recipe for Fat Youth," *New York Times*, September 19, 2000, F8.

3. Eric Nagourney, "For Exercise, Every Minute Counts," *New York Times*, September 25, 2000, F8.

4. Linda Marsa, "In Search of Sleep," *Child* (September 2000): 118.

5. Nancy Hellmich, "A Teen Thing: Losing Sleep," *USA Today*, March 28, 2000, 1A.

6. Kate Stone Lombardi, "Stresses and Strains of Backpacks," *New York Times*, February 16, 2000, B8.

7. Suggestions 4–6 were inspired by a story by Amy Fishbein, "Lighten Up," *Seventeen* (September 1999): 146.

8. Jane E. Brody, "Fresh Warnings on the Perils of Piercing," *New York Times*, April 4, 2000, F8.

9. Christine Fellingham, "Water Can Change Your Life," *O Magazine* (July–August 2000): 136.

CHAPTER ELEVEN

1. Michiko Kakutani, "Hold the Pickles, Hold the Lettuce," in a review of *Fast Food Nation: The Dark Side of the All-American Meal*, by Eric Schlosser, *New York Times*, January 30, 2000, E9.

2. Cindy Rodriguez, "Grade School Girls Gripped by a Fear of Being Overweight," *San Francisco Chronicle*, December 31, 1998, A4.

3. Jane E. Brody, "Increasingly, America's Sweet Tooth Is Tied to Sour Health," *New York Times*, September 21, 1999, F7.

4. Jane E. Brody, "Added Sugars Are Taking a Toll on Health," *New York Times*, September 12, 2000, F8.

5. Associated Press, "Extra Soft Drink Is Cited as Major Factor in Obesity," *New York Times*, February 16, 2001, available from nytimes.com.

6. Mindy Sink, "Losing Meat, but Keeping a Child's Diet Balanced," *New York Times*, July 25, 2000, D7.

7. Ibid.

8. Ibid.

9. Ibid.

10. Ibid.

CHAPTER THIRTEEN

1. Daniel S. Levy, "Too Early Too Young," *Time* (March 5, 2001): 78.